the Rhinebeck Sweater

this book belongs to:

TECHNICAL SUPPORT

Confused about something in one of the patterns, or have a question? The support page on my website contains links to useful resources, tutorials and frequently asked questions. **www.ysolda.com/support**

EBOOK

To access your download please visit **www.ysolda.com/redeem** and enter the unique code printed inside the back cover.

Photography: Ysolda Teague

Graphic Design: Julie Levesque, www.symposi.com

Technical Editor: Kristi Porter

Copy Editor: Jo Kelly

ISBN 978-0-9565258-5-7

MIX
Paper from responsible sources
FSC
www.fsc.org
FSC® C006060

Printed and bound in America by Puritan Capital on FSC® certified papers using vegetable based inks. www.puritancapital.com

Ysolda and friends
CELEBRATE SHEEP
AND WOOL

with

the Rhinebeck Sweater

a collection of

TWELVE SWEATER PATTERNS,
STORIES, AND MORE

Table of Contents

by Ysolda Teague

The New York State Sheep and Wool Festival — popularly referred to as Rhinebeck — has taken place on the third weekend of October at the Dutchess County Fairgrounds in Rhinebeck, New York since 1972. Now attracting more than 40,000 visitors over the weekend, it's a celebration of all things sheep and wool and a dream destination for knitters from all over the world.

I knew none of that when I first encountered the Rhinebeck sweater being discussed on blogs. The exact details didn't matter. What drew me in was the palpable excitement about knitting a sweater under pressure of a deadline, sharing your progress with lots of other people doing the same thing, and finally showing it off to people who would really get it. So often as knitters we worry that what we make might look a little too homemade, that it won't blend into the crowd, that we're wearing too many hand knits at once. Those concerns were irrelevant when choosing a Rhinebeck sweater: the most eye-catching showcase for the knitter's skills possible. I wanted to be part of that.

A few years later, when I finally crossed the Atlantic and made it to Rhinebeck myself, I was thrilled to find that I was already a part of the celebration. There was no greater honour than seeing that other people had chosen one of my patterns as their Rhinebeck sweater. I spent the weekend overwhelmed and excited; photographing everyone I saw wearing one of my designs, and every cute animal I could find.

The barns were filled with such an array of yarns, in fibres I'd never heard of before, and I wanted to try everything. Paralysed by indecision I came home with a random pile of single skeins, all of them delightful and ideal for the work I was doing on what would become the Whimsical Little Knits series. But I was left with a lingering sense of regret. Wouldn't it have been nice to make a Rhinebeck sweater in yarn from the festival? If only I'd committed to something.

Over the years my pile of precious skeins of souvenir yarns grew, gathered from visits to festivals, farms, dyers and other small producers all over Europe and North America. I loved dipping into that trunk for a special shawl or hat, but there is nothing I like knitting, or designing, more than sweaters. There was nothing in the trunk for that, and I found myself wishing that I'd bought a gift for my future self, as Clara Parkes so perfectly puts it. I wanted a sweater filled with happy memories, made from yarn with a fascinating story.

The Rhinebeck sweater I wore that first year wasn't a sweater at all. Ravelry meet-ups at Rhinebeck had become a gathering place for the community, a chance to meet online friends in real life, and, of course, to share what you'd knit.

(continue)

Knitters were excited to meet the team behind their beloved website, who had become good friends of mine, but they often asked where the mascot, Bob the Boston Terrier was. Pets aren't allowed at the festival, but I started to think that Bob needed a stand-in for public appearances. A week before Rhinebeck I'd given up on finishing a sweater but I had an idea. I was staying with Gudrun Johnston and her family and I dragged her and her kids around every craft and toy store in the area as I amassed black and white yarn, a plastic ball, paint, stuffing and wire. No one knew it was me inside the giant head and paw mittens, but everyone at the meet-up wanted to have their picture taken with Bob. It was one of my silliest ideas, but people really got it, and I knew then just how special this community of knitters I'd found myself among was.

This book, like most of my work, grew slowly out of conversations with other designers. It started years ago with the idea that it would be fun not just to knit Rhinebeck sweaters, but to team up and design them. It took five books, and a few years, before I felt like that was a project I could take on and I started casually mentioning the idea to friends. Fortunately they were as excited as I was, and the festival in 2012 was the perfect chance to do a photo shoot with everyone in the same place. It was important to me that the designers would model their own sweaters: I asked them to design the sweater they would want to wear and show off at the festival. The resulting garments are as beautiful as their happy smiles and I hope you'll want to show them off as well.

This book is centred around one festival, which might be local to you or unimaginably far away, but I hope it will encourage you to seek out others. The idea of shopping locally for yarn assumes that everyone has locally-made yarn available and that no one ever travels, but no matter where you live (or where you visit) you may be surprised by what is out there when you start looking. You might find a dyer with an instinctive colour sense, or a mill that's been in operation for decades. Maybe there's a shepherd who knows the whole flock by name, or a spinner who only sells at one farmers' market. The yarns will all be special to the people who made them, and they'll all have a story for you to continue. When you find them, I hope you won't be put off by a lack of pattern support, and that you'll fill your arms with enough to really do something with.

I knew this book had already started working its magic on me when I found myself running through Union Square, in Manhattan, last January. I was rushing back to my hotel to pick up my suitcase and catch a flight, but I suddenly remembered that it was Saturday and Catskill Merinos would have a booth at the market. A rapid change of direction and I grabbed an armful of yarn, roughly estimating a sweater quantity and adding two extra skeins for luck. The woman at the till tried to tell me about the yarn, a story I'd normally love to hear, but I thrust some notes at her with 'I know, I love it, I have to run.' She probably thought I was horribly rude as I ran across the square, but I couldn't stop grinning as I sat on the subway hugging my carrier bag full of wool — a future sweater.

That yarn is still waiting for my future self to discover it again, but when I do I know it will become a Rhinebeck sweater. It doesn't matter anymore whether it's actually worn to Rhinebeck, the important thing is to wear it somewhere with pride. Make something that you love, and that shows your love for knitting and for yarn. I hope that in the following pages you'll find the perfect pattern for your own Rhinebeck sweater.

ON STASHING, SNACKING, AND THE MERITS OF BUYING LOCAL

by Clara Parkes

In the summertime, my farmers' market bustles with activity. People come from miles around to squeeze the tomatoes, sniff the peaches, and peel back the tips of corn to see if the cob is good. When it is, they rarely plunk just one ear into their bag. No, they're thinking ahead and planning meals. Five, six, even a dozen ears are picked. A bushel of tomatoes is set aside. One peach goes down the hatch before they even get the rest back to the car.

There's nibbling and then there's planning a meal. I used to graze at fibre festivals much like I nibbled at farmers' markets, picking up one pretty tomato to gaze at longingly, perhaps a single skein of Mohair far too pretty to use. I went on this way for years, and I have a house full of single skeins to show for it. They're charming little appetizers, but they aren't a meal. Rarely will they get me anywhere beyond, say, a warm head or most of a cosy neck. When we progress from a swatch-like scarf to a complete sweater, arms and all, we advance from adorning to truly clothing ourselves.

Volume can be a beautiful thing. A bushel of ripe apricots yields countless jars of preserve to brighten up a February morning. A sweater's worth of yarn is an even more generous gift to your future self. Like the squirrel finding its acorn stash, one day you'll stumble upon this bag of yarn, fall in love with it all over again, and be so grateful that you had the foresight to buy enough that you could actually *do* something with it.

The farmers' market and fibre festival are fleeting in a way a grocery store or LYS will never be. No matter what the time of year, you know that your grocer will always have tomatoes. They may be plum or Beefsteak, canned, peeled, or frozen, and nobody can guarantee that they'll actually taste like anything, but they'll be there. Working on a pattern that calls for a workhorse worsted-weight wool? Chances are you'll find something suitable at your LYS.

But at the farmers' market and fibre festival, you have that sense of seasonality that brings urgency. Those cherries you're eyeing? They weren't airlifted from Argentina, they really came from Farmer McFadden's tree. (At which point Farmer McFadden looks up and waves at you.) And when they're gone, they're really, truly gone — at least for another year.

We love and need yarn stores because they will always stock the staples we need, and they can be our lifeline to the local knitting community. Fibre festivals augment our stashes with those exquisite, fleeting seasonal joys. They also bring us to people. To visit a fibre festival is to connect with those who actually "grew" your yarn. They don't stock the same product 365 days a year. They have a certain supply, and when it's gone, you'll have to wait for the sheep to grow more.

(continue)

With people come stories. Talk to the vendor and she'll be able to tell you about the sheep breed that produced the fibre in their yarn, how big the flock is, how moody or temperamental the animals. Was it a rough winter? Did lambing go well this year? Pop just one or two simple questions and a river of information quickly flows. Knowing more about where a yarn came from always deepens my experience of using it.

Don't get me wrong, I'm still a staunch supporter of yarn stores, and you'll often find me nibbling on single skeins to tide me over until the next meal. Those single skeins always tell me something, teach me something about twist or ply or technique that I may not have otherwise known. They keep my fingers nimble and my mind alert so that when another truly exceptional yarn reveals itself, I'll know, in that way you *know*, that this is the real deal.

Every year, I end my fibre festival season with a visit to the New York Sheep and Wool Festival in Rhinebeck. The leaves are beginning to turn, the pumpkins are ripe, nostalgia is in the air. It's my last chance to stock up before the long Maine winter, so stock up I do.

When I stumble upon a great yarn during my travels, I'll confidently sock away more of it than would require an average sweater my size, adding an extra skein for good measure — perhaps that sweater will want a hat, or fingerless mitts, or maybe both? I stash because these are not anonymous skeins among thousands of identical ones. They're unusual skeins from smaller homes, with deeper roots and more colourful stories.

The economical impact of your investment nourishes those roots. In buying directly from producers, you're putting money directly into the community in which they live — toward everyone from the shearer to the vet or the guy who comes once a year to trim the flock's hooves.

Something as simple as the purchase of some yarn enables a person to pay property taxes and ultimately preserve a community's green space. I've even seen cases where a single hand-dyer generates enough volume to keep her community's post office open. Does that person have a family? Children who attend a school? The impact of your investment, its positive ripple effect, only broadens.

> ❝ *I stash because these are not anonymous skeins among thousands of identical ones. They're unusual skeins from smaller homes, with deeper roots and more colourful stories.* ❞

As noble as it may be to help preserve communities, that's not the *real* reason why we buy yarn, right? No, we're supporting small producers because their yarn called to us. It's special, and in its uniqueness we spot an opportunity for us to express ours.

Jenny at the Fair

by Mary Jane Mucklestone

EVERY YEAR RHINEBECK CREEPS UP and surprises me. Suddenly I need a sweater that is both fun and fast to knit, and comfortable no matter what the weather brings. A gently fitted colourwork cardigan hitting just below the bum was this year's solution. It's cute and swingy unbuttoned for warm weather, perfectly comfy when buttoned, and has just enough ease for additional layering should temperatures plunge. The V-neckline is smart and cool on its own, yet invites a scarf or cowl for added warmth. Lively, easy-to-memorize colourwork patterns flow into an even easier peerie pattern for the upper body and raglan yoke. Sneaky pockets for stashing vendors' cards offer a wee jolt of unexpected colour. Nash Island yarn makes the garment perfect. It is thick enough to make the work go quickly, yet lofty, so although the sweater is long, it is light as a feather! Jani, the colour wizard of Starcroft Fiber, has developed a gorgeous colour palette: all the shades look lovely together no matter what the combination, making it simple to customize your own version of this sweater.

Worked from the bottom up, the lower body ribbing is worked back and forth in rows, and then joined with centre front steek stitches for working in the round, making the colourwork sections easy and fun to knit. Sleeves are knit in the round up to where they are joined with the sweater body. Then the yoke is worked in the round. V-neck shaping and raglan armhole shaping are worked simultaneously. When the body is complete, the steek is reinforced with a line of slip-stitch crochet, and cut down the centre ... not to fear! This is a great first project for steeking. The sweater is finished with a ribbed button band.

Pattern directions on *page 114.*

OXO
MARY JANE

'Come early, stay late,
be patient and have fun…'
— *Chris Roosien*

MARY JANE MUCKLESTONE

Someone asked me recently if Mary Jane is always smiling. When we visited Nash Island for the shearing she had a sinus infection. Even so she was making jokes about the novelty of getting one for the first time, grinning while scooping up armfuls of sheep shit. The day after the shearing, as I was stretching sore muscles, Mary Jane jumped up, swallowed a painkiller and talked me into hiking. We climbed the Beehive in the Acadia National Park, essentially a cliff face with some steel hand-holds, but absolutely worth the breathtaking views.

Mary Jane's design work has focused on stranded colourwork — Jenny at the Fair is a perfect example — and her book 200 Fair Isle Motifs is one of my favourite references. She also puts her wonderful eye for combining colours and patterns to work as a stylist on photo-shoots for Twist Collective, Quince and Co. and Interweave Knits.

Ravelry: MaryJane
www.maryjanemucklestone.com

STARCROFT FIBER MILL

At 7am we gathered at the dock: shearers, mill owner, a doctor moonlighting as a shepherd, a herd of teenagers, and assorted friends and family. In the bright early morning sunshine we loaded crates of equipment, coolers, and a cast iron kettle into lobster boats and set off on an annual excursion that's been made for nearly a century. Our destination was a small island, Big Nash, off the down-east coast of Maine (actually, rather far to the North, but when it was named the prevailing winds that brought the shipping traffic from Boston were downwind).

In 1916 a small girl, Jenny Purington (later Cirone), made this same short journey aboard the tender Hibiscus to the smaller of the two Nash islands, Little Nash, where her father was to be the lighthouse keeper. Growing up on the island, Jenny kept lobster boats, helped to polish the lighthouse bell, cared for the family's livestock and went to school intermittently whenever a teacher visited. Jenny described why the teachers never lasted long: 'Then she'd go home and one of my brothers'd propose. That's what kept happenin to 'em. My seven brothers took to marryin 'em fast as they come on the island.'

There is a long history of keeping sheep on islands; there are dozens of islands along the coast of Maine named 'Sheep or Ram Island'. Most are now nothing but a curiosity on the map, but thanks to Jenny the tradition thrives here. As children, Jenny and her siblings played with the sheep, riding them like horses and using them to haul coal to the house. When she married and moved to the mainland, Jenny continued to care for the sheep; over the following years she bought up

(continue)

all of the land on the islands that didn't belong to the government. For seventy years, Jenny Cirone captained her own lobster boat and raised her sheep. Before she passed away in 2004, Jenny entrusted the sheep to her friends and neighbours, Eleni and Alfie Wakemen, who had helped with lambing and shearing over the years. The youngest of the Wakemen's three daughters, who is playing with the friendly bottle-raised lambs when we arrive on the island, is named for Jenny.

The days leading up to the shearing have been filled with anxiety about the weather. Jani Estell, owner of Starcroft Fiber Mill, has been trading daily phone calls about the forecast with Alfie. They joke that he used to mock Jenny's nervous weather watching, but that she almost always picked a perfect date. Visiting from Scotland, in between two work events, this is the only weekend I can be here. The night before the shearing I arrive at Jani's with Mary Jane Mucklestone, designer of Jenny at the Fair, and a couple of other knitting friends, including photographer Gale Zucker who is shooting the shearing for a local magazine. Jani and her husband Grant recently packed up their respective mills, hers a high-tech mini spinning mill, his a sawmill, and moved from Western Maine to be closer to the sheep.

The mill is up and running in a giant trailer, they're living in a temporary small house, there's a caravan for visitors, and, around pillars of beautiful forked trees, Grant is building a new house. There's no running drinking water, and connecting to the internet is impossible, but the adorable outhouse has a wonderful view. Most importantly, the dock is only a short drive away; earlier in the spring Jani and the Wakemens spent the few weeks of lambing season practically living on the island.

We go to bed nervously watching the cloudy sky. There's a last phone call with Alfie: the shearing is on, but uncertain. In the night I wake to raindrops on the caravan's metal roof. A comforting sound, until I remember where I am. If it's raining, the shearing will be called off — it sounds obvious, but until now I'd never thought about the fact that you can't shear wet sheep.

This morning is clear, blue skied, and perfect. When we get to the island, the only effect of the weather is a break

with tradition — to give everything a chance to dry out in the rapidly warming sunshine, we'll eat breakfast before the work of rounding up the sheep. On the island is a small camp, a cozy shingled cabin with kitchen and bunkroom. The kitchen volunteers, and everyone who's contributed to the breakfast and lunch pot-lucks, take the job of feeding the three shearers very seriously. Later, at lunch, we'll line up strictly in order of job difficulty from shearers on down. For now, we fuel up on a vast spread of egg casseroles, muffins, and fresh doughnuts.

Before the roundup, Alfie gathers us in a huddle, splits us into teams, and stresses that no one wants to do this more than once: pretend you're a bush and don't spook the sheep into scattering. In Jani's group, my job is simple: to hide near the camp, ready to creep up and help funnel the sheep into the pen. Other groups head off in the opposite direction, to circle the island, gathering the sheep in front of them as they go. As we creep through the wildflower-covered bog, a landscape so close to the Scottish Highlands that it feels intimately familiar, we crouch low, carefully avoiding gulls' nests full of speckled eggs and occasional huddles of pom-pom like chicks. The birds assault us with their harsh cacophony, flying in dips that pass a hair's breadth above our heads. Throughout the day it will be obvious, from the crowd of angry gulls, when someone has snuck off to pee.

Over a hummock the flock appears, their herders following slowly on three sides, arms held out widely. Closest to us is the rangy figure of Donna, one of the shearers, a woman in her sixties whose strength I envy. Calmly, she creeps behind the sheep, directing her team with hand signals to duck down, to move faster. We move forward, creating the last line of humans that will funnel the sheep into the first of a series of wooden pens. The roundup, careful and slow, has been a success. Inside the pen, where I find myself, the pace picks up.

The eldest of the Wakemen girls grabs a lamb from the back of the pen and thrusts it towards me. Its weight and strength are a surprise, and I struggle to hold it firmly as I hand it over the fence to a waiting pair of arms. It takes a strong kick in the face before I learn to hold their legs

(continue)

down. We work quickly, searching between the press of bodies for the smallest lambs. It's important to remove them, in case they're trampled in the confines of the pen. The lambs will be checked over, their tails docked, and the males castrated — a relatively simple process of applying rubber bands — before they're released to wait, bleating for their mothers.

Now the day's real work begins. Cloths are spread on the ground, a portable generator set up, and the three shearers line up. The tops of cloth bags are rolled down, ready to receive the fibre, and a table is set up for skirting. A few sheep are split from the main group, into a smaller pen from which the teenagers will wrestle them over to the shearers, one by one. The three women, including Eleni Wakemen, huddle over the sheep, using their whole bodies to expertly manoeuvre them. The belly first, the sheep on its back, leaning on the shearer's legs — they exclaim over clean, almost hairless bellies, moan about the ones that are matted thickly with mud. Around the tail, and the sheep is rolled so the back can be sheared; a volunteer reaches gloved hands in to pull away the worst of the shit.

Mary Jane has been bragging about her skills as a shit picker; she's positively gleeful when the sheep is a particularly productive one. Later in the day I learn that

it's all in the timing, to avoid interrupting the shearer's smooth progress, not to pull on any fibre that's still attached which could cause the skin to be nicked by the whirring blades. Surprisingly, it's not particularly disgusting; I quickly abandon the sweaty gloves in favour of scrubbing well afterwards.

Jani flits about between each batch of three, examining fibre between her fingertips. When the last fibres are separated, close to the neck, the naked sheep is released to spring back to the pen and we gather the fleece, cut side out, and thrust the bundle up to the skirting team. Jani calls out the grade of the fleece, the finest are reserved for handspinners, the majority already sold on the reputation of previous years. The coarsest, shortest fleeces, usually those from the oldest sheep, will end up as felt, and the majority will be used for Jani's yarn. All of the wool for her yarn comes from the island sheep.

The last sheep of the day is troublesome, her shearer still working methodically while the other two have thrown themselves full length in the dust, resting in the sun that has beaten on their backs all day. The fleece, when it's finally off, turns out to be almost completely felted. Difficult to shear, the fibres had to be teased apart slowly. But this provides the answer to a question I've often wondered about. Wool, it turns out, can felt on the sheep. Not the result of a too

hot bubble bath, but a reaction to extreme stress. Alfie speculates that she may have lost a lamb.

The sheep are mainly a Coopworth-Romney blend, although Jenny, apparently, was grateful for any sheep sent her way. Over the last few years, Jani and the Wakemens have made careful attempts to improve the quality of the fibre, but many of their experiments have resulted in disaster, and a new respect for doing things 'the way that Jenny did them'. Introducing a Shetland ram was a particularly bad idea. Although the landscape looks similar to the even more remote Shetland Isles, the winters are much colder, Shetland lambs are small, and not all survived the spring weather. To keep the flock healthy, a new ram is introduced every two years, to avoid breeding the ram with his daughters. Our final job, on leaving the island today, is to drop the two rams off to spend the summer on their own lonely island, the Ladle. Since the timing of lambing season to avoid the harshest weather is so crucial, they won't be brought back to the flock until December.

We tie up the sacks of wool, pack away the remnants of lunch, wind up cables, and haul everything back down the pebbled beach. Wading out, many hands thrust the sacks onto Donna's small boat, with which she ferries everything — people, supplies, wool — out to the waiting lobster boats. There's just time to feed a bottle to a lamb and snuggle a little before we wave goodbye.

Back at the mill we unload the haul, hoisting each sack up to be weighed with machinery usually used for logs. Some of the sacks are close to a hundred pounds. We wrestle them through the doorway and pile them high in the mill. Jani has a busy summer and winter ahead of her, cleaning, spinning and dyeing this soft, 'fog-washed' fibre. Exhausted, muddy, and a little sun burnt, I take a bath sitting in one of the huge mill sinks. It isn't long before my clean hair is filled with the scent of woodsmoke, but the logs on the campfire have been carefully selected for their fragrance, and we roast hot dogs and marshmallows as we reminisce about our perfect day, and hear stories of other, not so perfect shearing days.

Starcroft's special Nash Island Wool yarns are produced in small quantities. Before the move that necessitated shutting down production for almost a year, Jani had been selling the yarn at local fibre festivals, and was considering Rhinebeck. Although the yarn cannot currently be found at the festival, I was fascinated by its story, and look forward to seeing it there one day. In the meantime, it can be ordered online, and found in a small number of Maine yarn stores.

'My tips are kind of like basic hiking tips. Dress in layers for all weather eventualities. Bring water — you don't want to be delirious with dehydration while perusing the yarn selections. Emergency food, the lines can be long, and you need to stave off cranky. I find a light day pack is useful, so I have my hands free to fondle the yarns, eat artichokes and pet the sheep, not to mention store all the yarn and books I purchase (avoid large backpacks that can hit people in the crowds though!) Comfortable shoes or boots- you'll be doing lots of walking and standing, and nothing precious — ones you don't mind getting trashed in the mud or around the animals.'

— *Mary Jane Mucklestone*

Dutchess

by Cheryl Burke

DUTCHESS IS A WORSTED-WEIGHT PULLOVER knit with generous decorative ribbing and waist shaping for a more flattering fit. The herringbone colourwork yoke is simple to remember, fun to knit, and uses only two colours. With minimal finishing, you'll be off to Rhinebeck in warmth and style!

Dutchess has a simple construction to show off the bold colourwork design. The body and sleeves are worked in the round to the armholes, then joined for the circular yoke. Short rows are used to raise the back of the neck after the sleeves and body are joined. The yoke and neckband are worked in the round.

Pattern directions on page 120.

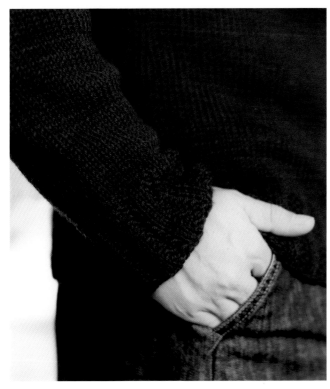

CHERYL BURKE

I first met Cheryl in the grey car park of a strip mall near her home in Western Massachusetts, on the way to Rhinebeck. She was already waiting with her husband when we pulled up, and seeing her from a distance it was as though the festival had already begun — a beacon of brightly coloured, woolly cheer in the dreariest of locations. Cheryl specializes in simple sweaters in lively colour combinations, you might have seen her patterns published by Twist Collective or Berroco.

Ravelry: yarnbee

SHELRIDGE YARNS

Canadian designer and dyer Lyn Gemmell recently took over the well-established yarn company Shelridge Yarns, leaving behind the corporate world for a life dyeing yarn in a barn in rural Ontario. I asked her about the company, how she became involved in it, and their experiences at Rhinebeck.

How did Shelridge begin?

The company began approximately twenty years ago when Buffy and Don Taylor kept a flock of sheep at their Ontario home, Shelridge Farm. Buffy had the fleeces spun into yarn and dyed it herself. She sold the yarn directly from the farm and at the few sheep and wool shows then around. Demand for Buffy's glorious colour grew so fast that she and Don had a local mill spin yarn to their exacting standard, Buffy continuing to dye it. Shelridge was an early booth-holder at Rhinebeck, making the all-day drive from rural Ontario to Dutchess County every autumn.

And how did you come to buy the business?

My involvement with knitting design began about twenty-five years ago. I was living a corporate life in the UK, and once a summer I would return to my family's camp on the north shore of Lake Huron. My sister Deb taught me to knit while we

(continue)

sat by the lake. We began designing together, and when I moved back to Canada from the UK we started Cabin Fever to publish our patterns. We also carry other people's yarn and I have done a lot of dyeing for Cabin Fever. When I bought Shelridge Yarn about a year ago, we spent nearly all the transitional time with Buffy teaching me to dye yarn in the Shelridge way, which I continue to do.

Tell me a little about the scale of your business. Do you have employees, or people who help you do events like Rhinebeck?

Shelridge Yarns remains a small independent dyeing business. I do the dyeing personally, every time, in a dye barn behind our house in Ontario. Managing a small business like Shelridge feels directly related to both parts of my working life: as a designer and, before that, as a partner in a large international consultancy and accountancy firm. I also try to remember how we advised small business owners to delegate. There are six or seven people that I rely on to help me with particular parts of the Shelridge business. At Rhinebeck, many shoppers look forward to seeing Buffy, who still works with me and loves to attend a few of her (and my) favorite shows. Rhinebeck tops that list.

How has the business changed over the years? What has it been like to combine your two businesses?

As a business, Shelridge has grown rather than changed. More yarns to choose from and many, many more rich colours, but all dyed with the same methods and formulae developed by Buffy Taylor.

For me, owning both Shelridge and Cabin Fever, there have been many adjustments. My family can tell you how much more time I spend away from phone and computer while I am in the dye barn. In my pre-Shelridge days, I might do some proofreading in the evening, but generally I left my desk at the end of the day. A small yarn business takes up a huge amount of space! There is yarn all over the office and the house. Skeining and labeling and swatching and many other tasks happen at odd hours and in many parts of the house.

Can you tell me a bit about your dyeing process?

There are lots of words used with the artisan style of yarn production (versus the large commercial mills). Words like 'kettle dyeing', 'hand dyeing' and so forth. I'm not actually completely sure what everyone means by some of these terms or even if we mean the same things. For my 'solid' colours (or some people say 'semi-solids') I dye in the skein or hanks. By that I mean I skein the yarn first, then dye the skeins in a big pot, generally for 90 minutes per batch. The yarn is then washed and hung to dry. Once dry, I twist them back into tidy skeins and label them — usually while watching TV at night. My husband does the majority of the labeling which is a great help, except for his whining when it comes to pink. He's such a guy.

Hand-painted yarns are done on a big table with dye in squirt bottles (like you see for mustard at hot dog stands). They're steamed to set the dye without disturbing the colours. It's fun and quite interesting to see what you end up with. I really enjoy having hand-painting workshops in the barn to see the beautiful colour combinations people create.

Creating new colours is complex and often frustrating; and sometimes it's surprisingly easy, or even accidental. I recently came up with a new colour that I'm testing out to see if other people like it as much as I do. It was the result of grabbing the wrong dye colour when mixing up a combination of dyes. When I realised what had happened I was already pouring it into the dye pot. So I went with it.

Do you think about what the yarn will become while you're working on it? As a designer I can imagine it's a bit dangerous.

I often find myself falling in love with colours each time I dye them. You have no idea how many projects I've started with a colour just after I've dyed it again — many of which are not finished! When people order yarn I wonder what they'll do with it. Many people actually let me know what they're planning on knitting or crocheting, which I really appreciate, but if they don't I try to figure out by the colours and quantities they've ordered. I love it when people send me pictures of what they've knit. Which again causes me to cast on yet another project … I do suffer from 'startitis'!

What makes your yarn unique? Can you tell me more about the Soft Touch W4 that Cheryl used for Dutchess?

Clearly I totally love the yarn and am completely biased but I think the hand of the yarn is fantastic. I've recently added a number of new colours to the W4 line and expect that will continue over the next couple of years. As a knitter, I think the yarn itself has a wonderful 'bounce' or life to it. It has great body and feels terrific while you're working with it as well as wearing the finished garment. I've not seen or worked with another yarn quite like it. The original range of colours developed by Buffy work beautifully when combined in techniques like Fair Isle. The profile of the yarn and the harmonious palette allow muted and subtle combinations as well as vivid contrasts.

From your events schedule it looks like you try to get to as many shows and festivals as possible. What does selling your yarn in person offer that you can't get online?

I live just outside a village of 900 people, with no neighbours to speak of near my house. Most of my communication is by email or phone. I love shows. I get to talk to people in person. People who share my obsession. Who love to talk about yarn and projects and colours and combinations and thoughts and ideas. It's heaven. Plus I get to meet up with old friends who are also there for the show or festival. Bonus!

It's always interesting to talk to people in person — the internet and communities such as Ravelry are great — but nothing is as interesting or helpful as face to face time. You can't get the excitement, the enthusiasm, or the light in their eyes as they're talking from the internet. Living in the country, surrounded by fields full of corn and cows, it's great to be able to talk to a lot of people all with the same interests. I think it's helpful for our customers too, to meet and talk, ask questions and get answers.

Seeing colours in person? No photograph or computer screen can replace the tactile and visual impressions of seeing and touching the yarn, sample garments and looking at the colours.

I love seeing what the festival goers have chosen to knit or crochet and then wear to the show. Especially at Rhinebeck, people make a point of wearing their 'best.' At shows I have seen my first live examples of some designs and thought, 'a-ha, that shawl looks so much better in person than the images made it appear. Have to knit one of those, too!'

What is your experience of the festival like, from behind-the-scenes?

Both Buffy and I really love doing festivals and sheep and wool festivals are the most fun! We look forward to coming. Of course there is also the walking around and looking at all the animals and seeing the various displays. We loved the maple cotton candy last year. Only one person can be out of the booth at any given time so we take turns enjoying the festival, meeting friends and doing a bit of shopping. And, of course, we eat lamb at least one or two times a day. Yum.

Challenges include the weather: it can be very cold and very, very wet — last year our jeans were wet up to the knees after a walk around. We pack more clothes for this festival than any other: winter boots, galoshes, shoes, extra socks, heavy coats, light coats, vests, and, of course, sweaters.

Rhinebeck tends to bring many of the same vendors back year after year, and it feels like Old Home Week — *a tradition in many rural communities where former locals return home for a week of festivities* — during set-up as we see friends not seen for a year. It's our time to go out and catch up over a meal after the day is over. Plus knowing each other helps if you forgot something. Tape, price stickers, staples: there is always someone who has it to share.

The W4 yarn which Cheryl used for Dutchess shows that small batch, hand dyed, made in North America yarns come in all flavours: much as I love the rustic, sheepy variety, sometimes you need something a little slicker. A smooth, bouncy worsted-spun with great stitch definition, W4 can be machine washed, and gives a crisp appearance to Cheryl's geometric colourwork.

●

'At the shows we go to, I think the most satisfied folks come with a list and a plan. They have a list of projects that they want to do, with the yarn requirements for each. And they have a map of the facility and know where they are going and in what order.'

— *Miss Babs*

Sugarleaf

by Mary-Heather Cogar

DREAMING UP MY RHINEBECK SWEATER

has become one of my favourite fall rituals each year, and I always want to wear a warm and sturdy cardigan at the festival. The New Mexico Organic and Local Color by Green Mountain Spinnery, which are dyed and un-dyed versions of the same cosy woolen-spun base yarn, ended up providing the perfect outer layer for a chilly weekend outside. Sugarleaf is a versatile sweater with a modern, fitted silhouette that works as well in my "real life" as it does on a special wool festival trip. As I was working on Sugarleaf in preparation for my trip, it was such a pleasure to think of the yarn's origins: the sheep the wool comes from are raised just a few hours away from my home in New Mexico.

Sugarleaf's body is worked back and forth in one piece, from the top's face-framing circular yoke colourwork section down. Sleeves are picked up after the body is worked and knit seamlessly from underarms to the cuff. The cuffs and hem are trimmed with a garter rib, and a simple I-cord bind-off along the fronts and neck of the cardigan makes a tidy edging. Melissa Jean Design toggle buttons made from rich, smooth rosewood strike a lovely balance between rustic and sophisticated.

Pattern directions on *page 125.*

Mary-Heather

MARY-HEATHER COGAR

I've been to Rhinebeck every year since 2009, and every year I've
rented a house with a group of friends, including the Ravelry team.
Sheep and wool festivals don't tend to be near lots of hotels, so
this is an excellent option if you have a group — it's often cheaper
per person and gives you space to hang out. Mary-Heather
spends her days working with Ravelry advertisers and organising
events, but at Rhinebeck she combines her organisational skills
with her interest in cooking to make sure we're all well fed. She's
spent a decade working in the knitting industry: before joining
the Ravelry team, Mary Heather was manager of The Knit
Café in Los Angeles, where she honed her pattern writing skills
based on feedback from customers and students. Mary Heather
currently lives in Albuquerque, so the New Mexico Organic used
in Sugarleaf was the perfect fibre for her. Best of all, it means she
always shows up at Rhinebeck with her suitcase laden with jars of
green chilli sauce and corn tortillas: migas morning has become as
crucial a part of my Rhinebeck experience as the yarn shopping.

Ravelry: rainydaygoods
www.rainydaygoods.com

GREEN MOUNTAIN SPINNERY

When we first began working on this project, I asked the designers to submit design ideas and yarn suggestions. The yarn lists varied, but almost everyone had one from Green Mountain. In the end, I loved two of their yarns so much that I couldn't choose between them, and both got to stay. Both yarns are wonderful, both designers have a personal connection — Mary Heather lives in New Mexico where the fibre for her yarn is grown; Gudrun's home in Massachusetts is a short drive from where the yarn is spun — but the decision had more to do with the spinnery itself. It's a story that's at the heart of what I wanted to highlight with this book.

As I chatted with yarn makers, a few common threads started to emerge, one of which was that by and large their businesses had grown out of a hobby. Two of the four founders of Green Mountain Spinnery, Claire Wilson and Libby Mills, were professional weavers, disappointed by the lack of locally produced natural fibre yarns. The spinnery, however, was started very intentionally with the twin goals of sustaining the local economy and reducing environmental impact: focusing on yarn was a carefully thought out solution to several problems.

Inspired by E. F. Schumacher's *Small is Beautiful: Economics as if People Mattered* Claire and Libby, along with David Ritchie and Diana Whale, set out to create a small business that would use intermediate technology to support existing local production and generate employment within their community. In the late 1970s many New England dairy farmers were

(continue)

THE RHINEBECK SWEATER | 37

replacing their herds with sheep, but the wool wasn't being processed locally. At the same time, the yarns that the weavers were finding in local stores were imported, or were synthetics, something which seemed absurd during a fuel crisis.

Claire, David, Diana and Libby approached starting the spinnery methodically: writing a business plan, talking with local shepherds and visiting mills both near and far, including in Ireland and Wales. Their local community demonstrated their support in material terms: funding came from both formal agencies and friends and neighbours. At the time it would be the smallest woollen mill in the country, and maintaining the small scale of the business was central to the founders' philosophy. In keeping with the spirit of 'as if people mattered' the business is structured as a workers' co-operative.

Visiting Green Mountain Spinnery for the first time was a little surprising. Turning off Interstate 91 towards Putney, Vermont, the sign for the mill is immediately visible, but seems out of place. Although they looked at historical mill sites in the centre of Putney, none were just right, and the spinnery ended up housed in an abandoned gas station. Although it lacks the charm of the historical mills, the exterior is a good reminder that the spinnery is not about nostalgia or appearances: it's a functional working space.

Anyway, there's plenty of charm on the inside, where vintage machines are perfectly arranged to fit the small space. One of the major initial challenges in starting the spinnery was identifying, and then locating, the machinery that would create the kinds of yarns they wanted. The goal was to create minimally processed yarns that would retain the natural characteristics of the fibre while being reliably consistent and bouncy. From nearby Harrisville Yarns they received practical support and connected with employee Ray Phillips, a lifelong mill technician who offered to help them locate the equipment. They gathered their motley collection for picking, carding, spinning, plying, and skeining from textile mills all over New England. In one corner there's a beautifully patina'd brass and steel vessel: a washing machine from the laundry of an old hotel.

The mill finally opened in December 1981, with a yarn store at the entrance. They learned how to make yarn on the job and it wasn't long before Ray came on board to help full time. Practice makes perfect and over the years they've learned not only how to make classic yarns with vintage equipment, but have developed many innovative techniques. The GREENSPUN line of yarns are washed and spun with vegetable-based, rather than petroleum, oils and soaps, a process originally developed for a client, the clothing company Esprit. The process means that organically farmed fibre, such as the New Mexico Organic used by Mary Heather for Sugarleaf, can be spun into an entirely organically produced yarn. Jill Draper, who has some of her yarns spun by the spinnery, also highlights the importance of such environmentally friendly practices to her business.

My tour of the mill began with a visit to the shed, a grey wooden structure attached to the main building that's filled to the rafters with wool. Curly dark locks spill over the side of a plastic bag, burlap sacks are piled haphazardly, white fluff pokes out of holes in a stack of cardboard boxes. The wooden floor is covered not in dust bunnies, but with a tiny herd of sheep. Every natural hue of wool found in the fields is here, but climbing the loft I notice a mountain range of eye-searingly bright piles of fibre. The vibrant colours will become much more muted once blended and spun.

Some of the wool in the shed will go into the spinnery's own range, but many of the bags and bins are carefully labelled with the name of a shepherd or farm. They'll be kept together as they're passed from hand to machine and returned as roving or finished skeins. Supporting other businesses is central to the spinnery's founding mission and they work with breeders to create custom yarns that are ideally suited to their fibre, and can provide a valuable income stream for the farms. The spinnery is relatively small, but in *The Green Mountain Spinnery Knitting Book*, Margaret Klein Wilson writes: 'the Spinnery's sense of the whole, as a bridge between agriculture and knitting, extends well beyond what is happening at the mill'. In many ways the spinnery might be better described as a

(continue)

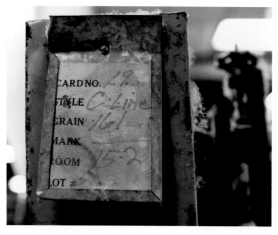

hub than a bridge: connecting farmers, yarn companies and knitters locally and further afield. When Gudrun and I talk about Scotland they tell us about encouraging the founders of a new mill in remote North Uist that shares many of the spinnery's community focussed goals.

Green Mountain Spinnery have been attending Rhinebeck for many years. Maureen Clark recalls sleeping in their cars at the first shows she attended: 'we have always had a wonderful time at Rhinebeck. Whether it snows, is a downpour for two days, or even in 95 degree heat, everyone is always happy to be surrounded by knitters and craftspeople. We used to camp out in our cars when I first started attending the show; it was like a big sleep over with lots of friends.'

With the on-site shop, frequent shows and an annual 'wool weekend' with a guest teacher hosted at the spinnery, direct interaction with knitters is important to Green Mountain. It was customer feedback that led to the development of their most recent yarn, Weekend Wool, which Gudrun used for Pippin. For many years its predecessor, Wonderfully Wooly, had been a staple of the Green Mountain line: a sturdy, rustic worsted wool in heathered colours. A great yarn that's proven popular for cosy outerwear, many customers wished it was softer, for wearing next to sensitive skin. At the same time the colour palette lent itself towards colourwork. Large four ounce skeins were appealingly bouncy, but off-putting when shopping for multiple colours for smaller projects.

The new yarn is a response to both of these issues. A carefully balanced blend of fine, soft wools, including Targhee, and more lustrous fibres like Corriedale, it looks almost exactly like Wonderfully Wooly but has a softer, bouncier hand that's a joy to work with, without being so soft that wearability becomes a concern. The most popular colours have been continued, alongside several new, contemporary additions. The skeins are also smaller, so closer to the right amount for a project can be purchased. The yarns look so similar that we actually ended up switching them during the process of writing this book. The new one wasn't ready in time for Gudrun to work with, so her sweater is photographed in Wonderfully Wooly, but once Weekend Wool was

available my assistant Rebecca knit a sample in it and it's the currently-available yarn that's used in the pattern. You'd never know from the photographs that they weren't in the same yarn and if you happen to have a stash of the discontinued one you could certainly use it here.

> 66 The yarn offers inspiration of its own, passing on its mantle of creativity to the next pair of hands. 99

I first discovered Green Mountain Spinnery through Kate Gilbert, editor of online magazine Twist Collective. Building mutually beneficial relationships with designers is important to the spinnery, and their yarns, as my experience with this book shows, have a particularly inspiring appeal to a lot of designers. Many of the people who work with the yarn every day find it equally inspiring and the co-operative has produced many in-house patterns over the years. They've also written two books featuring patterns and a behind-the-scenes look at the spinnery's work, in one of which the yarn's appeal is described thus: 'The yarn offers inspiration of its own, passing on its mantle of creativity to the next pair of hands.' Not only has Green Mountain Spinnery achieved their initial goals — of building a company that would support local businesses, provide local jobs and produce beautiful, environmentally friendly yarns — they continue to exceed them.

Pippin

by Gudrun Johnston

FALL IS MY FAVOURITE SEASON of the year and I love to have a good selection of basic sweaters to keep off the chill. When designing this garment I wanted to combine all of the elements of a sweater that make me happiest. This meant including a cowl, pockets, and nice long sleeves. Although the silhouette is simple, the unusual sleeve cap shaping keeps things interesting, while the cosy brioche stitch pattern adds texture.

Pippin is knit bottom up, beginning with a folded hem. The A-line shaped body divides at the underarms, and the front and back are worked flat. Increases are made at the outside edges of the front and back to create a modified drop shoulder or dolman type of sleeve without adding too much bulk at the underarm. The shoulder stitches are then grafted together. The sleeves are worked downward from stitches picked up around the armholes. The split cowl is worked by picking up stitches around the neck. The pockets are seamed to the sweater after finishing and are therefore easy to leave off if you desire.

Pattern directions on page 131.

GUDRUN JOHNSTON

Gudrun and I 'met' when she emailed me with some questions about pattern designing and publishing. At that point I'd been designing part-time for a couple of years. I'm not sure I knew any more than she did, but I was thrilled to chat with someone else doing the same thing. Gudrun now lives in Western Massachusetts, not too far from Rhinebeck and even closer to several of the yarn companies featured in this book. It wasn't long however before we realized quite how small the world is. Not only did we have a lot in common as new designers, but it turned out that we went to the same high school in her native Scotland. We were there at different times, but found plenty of common teachers to reminisce (complain) about. Since then, Gudrun and her family have put up with me invading their house with absurd large-scale craft projects and she's become one of the designers whose work I most admire.

Ravelry: Gudrun
www.theshetlandtrader.com

'Stay for Sunday afternoon if you can. It's quiet and mellower and relaxed towards the end of the day.'
— *Thea Colman*

'For first timers, I suggest that they get a program book and a pen and do a first walk around, marking who they'd like to go back to and spend more time. Obviously if you see something you love, go for it, but it's helpful to have a look around everything first. My other suggestion is that it can be overwhelming at first. Take breaks, sit down with a coffee or drink and relax and rest, and it's important to make sure you eat. Take it easy and enjoy!'

— *Lyn Gemmell*

Beekman Tavern

by Thea Colman

WHEN ASKED TO CONTRIBUTE TO THIS PROJECT, I immediately wanted to do a modern update to the classic Fisherman knit. It was an excellent excuse to knit with this gorgeous Cormo wool from Foxhill Farm. The resulting fabric is soft and round, with a bit of stretch to it, which gives the sweater a body skimming shape if knit with the suggested ease. I arranged the stitch patterns in a classic Fisherman's panel style but chose asymmetric cables for an unexpected, modern twist. Keeping detail outside of the main panel to a minimum reduces bulk. The double seed stitch panels on each side do allow you to play with shaping should you desire. Sleeves knit with only a slim cable keep things simple and streamlined. The ballet neckline is feminine and open, and the little button addition both draws the eye up and gives you an excuse to put a fun detail up on the collar. All in all, a softer, modern, and more flattering take on an old favourite.

Pattern directions on page 136.

THEA'S BEEKMAN COCKTAIL

Bourbon, Cointreau, and orange bitters. I fill the flask about 3/4 with bourbon, add about 1/4 of Cointreau and then shake bitters in a few times. As the day goes on I add it to the apple cider from the 4-H booth, and share with friends.

THEA COLMAN

After leaving a career in advertising to care for her daughters, Thea saved her sanity with knitting and get-togethers with neighbourhood friends for a drink before dinner, which they called 'babycocktails' because the cranky babies were the reason for the cocktails. The name eventually became her blog, where she posted about her knitting projects alongside cocktail recipes. Being unable to find exactly what she wanted to wear in stores led to her first designs. With catchy drink inspired names and classic designs with appealingly knitterly details, designing has become the perfect career to fit in around family life.

Quite a few knitters have told me they take a flask to Rhinebeck — an excellent idea, so I asked Thea to share what she puts in hers.

Ravelry: babycocktails
www.babycocktails.blogspot.com

FOXHILL FARM

Do any research into purchasing a Cormo fleece and it quickly becomes apparent that the name Alice Fields requires no further explanation: if the sheep in your flock were bred by her, the quality of their fibre is assumed. From Foxhill Farm in Lee, Massachusetts, Alice focuses on breeding sheep with exceptional fibre which she sells as fleece, processed fibre, and yarn at festivals like Rhinebeck. Foxhill Farm has no website and the yarns are available only at festivals — when it's gone it's gone — but it's well worth seeking out. The first time I went to Rhinebeck I eagerly asked everyone I encountered what the most exciting thing they'd found was: Foxhill Cormo was by far the most frequently mentioned.

I asked Alice how it all began: 'Quite some time ago my first sheep came to Foxhill Farm as a "gift" from 3 young 4-H'ers with a bottle lamb of dubious potential. But they said, "your cow needs a companion". And for many years she was just that, but also produced an annual bag of steel wool.' The sheep might have been an accidental addition to the farm, and her fleece rough, but for Alice it sparked an interest in fibre: 'I could spin steel wool!' The steel wool wasn't satisfying for long, however. 'When it came time for her to have new companions, the farm took on a new focus, initially with Romneys. And then with natural colored Romneys.'

Searching for finer fibre led to Cormo. 'As spinning and the various fiber arts became more popular, and my own interests more varied, so did the demand for finer fibers. My Cormo flock started with three animals.' Although they've become much more popular, those first three sheep were hard to find, but worth the effort.

In terms of the history of sheep breeding, Cormo is rather an interesting example: the breed was developed relatively recently, in the early 1960s, with a very scientific approach. Sheep geneticist Helen Newton Turner was commissioned by Tasmanian shepherd Ian Downie to help improve his flock. He was seeking larger, more fertile sheep and anticipating an increased demand for consistently high quality wool as buyers began to objectively analyse fibre. They introduced Corriedale rams, crossing them with his Saxon Merino ewes to create the new breed, the name of which is a contraction of Corriedale and Merino. The scientific approach extended to careful selection of the offspring to build the best breeding stock, with a focus on quality of fibre in addition to size and fertility. This initial approach can be seen in the current consistency of the breed, particularly in the diameter of the fibre, which must be extremely consistent throughout a single fleece. The fine wool can be as fine as 17 microns, as soft as Merino or even Cashmere, and has a regular, bouncy crimp pattern.

It was the quality of the fibre from those first three sheep that swayed Alice towards Cormo: 'Our first three fleeces were amazing! We gave these fleeces away — in 1 oz. bags to our loyal customers with the request that they "play" with it and give us feedback. And so, with overwhelming encouragement from our fiber friends, we grew a whole new flock.'

Alice loves the fibre, but breeding is an important part of her role as shepherd, and she continues the carefully considered approach to the Cormo breed. 'There is a real joy in raising quality animals. As a breeder one's job is to thoughtfully improve from one generation to the next. Many characteristics are important including lambing ease, mothering attitude, milking capacity, overall structure and longevity. Fiber length, crimp, density, consistency and fineness are also hereditary traits to consider in planning the next generations.

'Beautiful yarn is visual and tactile and it comes from somewhere you know, from people who care and animals that thrive. Cormo is exceptionally luxurious, soft and bright but also long stapled which makes it versatile for different styles of yarn. We have five different Cormo yarns ranging from lace weight to Aran. The yarns are full of life, airy and bouncy. The lace weight drapes beautifully and the heavier ones put a definitive pop to cables.'

The fibre from pure Cormo is the creamy white that recalls traditional Arans in Thea's Beekman Tavern, but Alice does play sorceress with the dyepots. Over the years she's also found that her love for natural colour was irrepressible and half the flock is now coloured Cormo crossbreeds. Alice explained that 'by always breeding back to Cormo rams, we have produced animals that are mostly Cormo in a full range of blacks, greys and moorit browns — and of course a comparable range of yarns. I love them all.'

> " Beautiful yarn is visual and tactile and it comes from somewhere you know, from people who care and animals that thrive. "

To ensure the cleanest, highest quality fleeces many farms, including Foxhill, choose to coat their flock: 'There is nothing more dazzling than "prime under coat" from a Cormo.' Coating takes considerable work. 'Each animal requires four to six coat changes a year to accommodate maturity, fleece growth, and pregnancies.' There is, however, less work at the end of the process: 'The coats protect the fleeces from the variables of weather and debris that can compromise their quality and color. Covered fleeces are easy to wash and process either by hand or commercially and have a high yield.'

For Foxhill Farm, festivals like Rhinebeck are an annual showcase. 'We get to show what's been happening on our farm all year — new yarns, new colors, new ideas, sheep news, etc. Actually it's always a "show and tell" both ways. So many of our customer-friends bring their projects to show us.' Alice is continually impressed and energized by the talent and loyalty of her customers, but their feedback also plays a crucial role in planning future yarns and fibres that will 'make us all happy.'

Alice's letter ended with what might be my favourite description of Rhinebeck: 'The Rhinebeck Festival is a real mecca for every type of fiber enthusiast and producer. It is such an opportunity for us all to enrich each other's fiber journey.' I know I always leave feeling full of possibility.

Pumpkin Ale

by Ysolda Teague

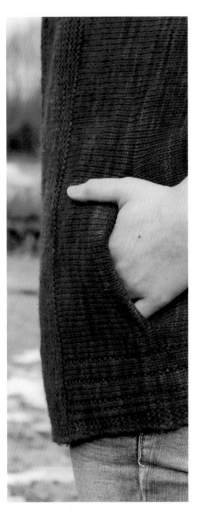

PUMPKIN ALE STARTED WITH A LIST: for Rhinebeck I wanted a versatile cardigan that could be worn open or closed; worn as a jacket, possibly even layered over a thinner sweater if the weekend was cool; pockets were a must for keeping change, business cards and a map handy; and the silhouette should be one that was easy to wear for many different body shapes.

Pumpkin Ale begins with a richly textured back panel that combines garter stitch and some of my favourite cable patterns. Working the panel by itself means that you can focus on the stitch pattern without worrying about shaping the rest of the sweater. Stitches are picked up down each side of the back panel and worked back and forth to create side panels that wrap around to form the front of the cardigan. The shaping within the back cable panel is combined with short rows at the sides to create a flattering flare from the waist. An edging pattern made up of only knit and purl stitches is worked simultaneously: simple but effective.

After joining the short shoulder seams, sleeve caps are shaped with short rows on stitches picked up around the armhole. The sleeves are worked in the round from the top down and feature a small cable pattern that echoes that on the back panel. The split cuff is worked back and forth, knit onto the live sleeve stitches.

A wide garter stitch band is worked on the live stitches from the fronts and stitches picked up around the back neck; an I-cord bind-off gives a neat finished edge. The neckband can be folded to create a collar or flipped up for extra cosiness when the day turns chilly. It wouldn't be autumn without some plaid flannel, so I used fabric to create the pocket linings; if you don't sew they could just as easily be knit.

Pattern directions on page 142.

MISS BABS

It's always a delight to visit the Miss Babs booth. Inside it's filled with beautiful yarn and a staff eager to help, and Babs herself — yes, there is a Miss Babs, the company name came from her husband, who uses it as a term of endearment — greets everyone with a smile so warm I always want to hug her.

Although she didn't start dyeing until 2003 it really all began with a move to the mountains of Tennessee a few years earlier. The move had the twofold effect of providing more time for Babs to 'experiment fully with the creative side of my world,' and of bringing her closer to nature, a continuing source of colour inspiration.

When she did learn to dye it was, fittingly, by taking a natural dye course at a local state park. 'We dyed with natural materials outside over fires in August. In spite of the heat, I was mesmerized by the magic of it all. I had already started playing with Kool-Aid and other food based dyes in my kitchen with yarn that I had spun.' At the time she was teaching marketing at a local university, but her weekends were spent outside, continuing to dye yarn over fires. 'I found some inexpensive wool yarn and bought it in bulk and dyed and experimented, and then started moving on to professional acid dyes. I created so much yarn, I had to find a way to sell it.' Babs started by supplying a friend's store, and, when her position at the university was phased out in 2005 she was able to transition to dyeing full-time. She quickly started selling online and at festivals: 'my first festival as a vendor was SAFF in October 2005 — Southeastern Animal Fiber Fair near Asheville, NC.'

(continue)

The 'About Us' page on the Miss Babs website proudly proclaims: 'It is a we, not just a me kind of business.' As the business has grown beyond her kitchen — and those outdoor fires — Babs has been 'blessed to find other like-minded women who like to work hard, are willing to do what needs to be done to get things done and like to enjoy ourselves with music and lots of talking while we do the work of the business.'

The process of growing the business and hiring new staff hasn't always been smooth, however. The most challenging period came when her husband was no longer able to work for health reasons. With greater financial pressure Babs found herself, 'working long days because I could not afford to hire additional people to do the work that had to be done.' The long days paid off and she was eventually able to hire more help, but this period continues to affect how seriously Babs and her team take this women-owned business: 'I had to crank the business up to create a living not only for us, but also for the women who work with me. Many of the women are either sole or significant providers for their households.'

> ❝ The color grew out of both my love of rich warm colors, and my experience in the culinary field. ❞

That team now consists of eight full-time members, 'and one part-time person who lives on the West Coast. I am the main dyer, but have an apprentice who is doing more of the dyeing as her skills expand. The business is based at my home. The studio used to be my husband's workshop, and we have now expanded that space this year because we needed more room!'

There have been plenty of other challenges along the way. Babs recounts how the pressures of preparing for a big show can mean a simple, very human, mistake can have big consequences. 'Three years ago I left a pot on the stove in the studio and it smoldered for over eighteen hours creating smoke damage. We lost ninety-five per cent of our completed inventory one month before a

major show. The yarn stunk and so it went into the dump. We went into overdrive to clean and repaint the studio, and get new stock in and dyed like crazy for three weeks and got to the show with a fair amount of inventory.' As someone who regularly burns things because I get distracted while cooking this story makes it very clear why I shouldn't consider a career change — I'd probably end up in this situation before every show, and I'm not sure I'd be as good at fixing it as the Miss Babs crew.

Babs herself continues to develop their colourways and colour is clearly a central part of her relationship with her environment 'I find the natural world of my surroundings is integral to who I am as an artist, the joy of the light on sunny days, the pleasure of seeing growing things change from bright spring greens to deeper summer greens, and then to deepest and muted fall greens tinged with browns. All these greens are surrounded by bright flower colors, clear blue skies, and grey foggy mornings.

'The development of most colorways starts through the mention of an idea, seeing a flower, or colors in nature, or a suggestion from Jen Jeffries who has been working with me for most of the time I have had the business. I then mull it in my mind's eye, thinking about it, how strong or light the color should be. This process can take a day or it can take a month or more. When I finally get to the mixing of the color, I usually have figured out the strengths and combinations of dyes that are needed to create what I want. The way the colors look in the knitting and crocheting is very important to us. Also very important to us is creating a broad range of colors and combination of colors.'

The colourway I used, Roasted Pumpkin, seemed like such a quintessential autumnal colour that I had to include it in this book. I asked Babs to tell me more about the inspiration behind the colour. 'You hit the nail on the head. I wanted a rich autumnal color to add to the palette of colors that we have. The color grew out of both my love of rich warm colors, and my experience in the culinary field.' — Babs's wildly varied resume includes a stint as a chef's apprentice. — 'I was envisioning caramelization, and soft but intense blended flavors of the roasted vegetable.'

Initially I swatched with a couple of other yarns from the Miss Babs line, but when she told me about Heartland I knew before even knitting with it that it would be perfect for this project. Babs explained how it came about: 'First of all, we have been looking to source a domestically grown and milled yarn for a number of years. We have also been looking for a non-superwash worsted weight Merino yarn to add to our line-up of yarn bases. This is driven by our desire to meet the needs of our customers. This difference broadens the choices for our customers with a different hand and feel.'

For me, the fact that it wasn't superwash, as most Merino yarns are, was a key reason for choosing Heartland for this design. Firstly, I wanted to stick with more natural yarns: making a yarn superwash involves either coating the fibres in a polymer resin, or burning off the microscopic scales in an acid bath. Secondly, from a design point of view, the superwash process changes how the resulting fabric behaves. The same scales that cause fulling when subjected to friction also help to hold the fibres in place against one another — it was important to me for this design that the garment would hold its shape well. Babs explained that the treatment, or lack of it, also affects the colour: 'Heartland, as a non-superwash yarn, takes dye and gives color back to your eye in a different way than superwash yarns.'

Even when there are no smoke damage incidents, preparing for one of the many shows Miss Babs attends every year means hard work for everyone. 'But most of that work happens in the two months or so before the show. And what happens at the show is the culmination and, hopefully, payoff for all that hard work you have done. We spend a lot of time planning the inventory for the booth so that our customers have tons to choose from in a layout that is easy to get around and that we can restock as the yarn is sold. We love the booth at Rhinebeck because it is the most spacious we have at any show. We realize that our customers are choosing to brave our sometimes crowded space, and we plan carefully to make it as pleasant as possible, with lots of samples for inspiration, and color galore for everyone's taste.'

Despite the work, Babs loves going to festivals, which might explain that smile: 'Going to festivals and being able to talk with customers and fans is one of the best parts! I love hearing about projects people are working on and making a personal connection with folks. Also, we've seen many of our customers over time and have found friends in many different areas of the country and from around the world. I think of SAFF as my "home show" since it was the first show I ever did and it is just two hours away. There is no doubt that the folks in the Southeast have been core supporters to my business, and for that I am very grateful. But I do love agricultural based festivals because they are comfortable and so friendly.'

Festivals can be a dramatic contrast to everyday life. 'At the show, we suddenly move from being in a studio in yucky dye clothes to being in show clothes and talking to customers about the yarn and projects and more. At Rhinebeck, we will have three of us from Tennessee, one gal who comes from the West Coast, and a friend from Massachusetts to do the set-up and work in the booth. We rent a house near town that has a hot tub, private rooms, a full bar, and that way we can have a little luxury at night. As hard as we work during the day we need a bit of comfort at night. Sometimes we eat out, usually Friday night at the Terrapin, but we also have food delivered so we can rest our feet.' It sounds like Miss Babs and her team have figured out exactly how to make sure everyone keeps smiling throughout the show, and, fortunately for us, how to go home with enough energy to dye more beautiful yarn.

'Don't overplan! I see too many stressed out festival-goers marching through with map in hand and a list of vendors to see, determined to buy nothing until they've seen everything, or else avoiding colours they love because they have too much of them, and then by the second time around they're exhausted, the colour they wanted is gone, or they've realised too late that they have a lot of blue because they really like blue. I think the key to festival enjoyment is spontaneity, checking out whatever booth strikes your fancy, and buying that blue skein when it speaks to you, even if your last three sweaters were all blue.'

— *Gryphon Corpus*

Aunt Fred

by Pamela Wynne

AUNT FRED IS MY
FAVOURITE KIND of sweater
to wear at a fall festival like Rhinebeck. It's
casual, colourful and warm, and it looks great
layered over a long-sleeved shirt.

As a proud Michigander, I chose to make
Aunt Fred with Briar Rose Fibers' Nate's Yarn.
It's a sport-weight yarn with a slightly slubby
texture that adds a sort of rustic quality to the
simple colourwork pattern.

The stranded colourwork pattern is inspired
by the curtains that hung in Aunt Fred's
avocado-and-goldenrod kitchen, which
existed as a 1970s time capsule until the
day she died in 2008. The construction
is seamless: the body and sleeves are knit
separately, then the upper body is worked
in a single piece, with set-in sleeves that are
shaped as you go.

Pattern directions on page 150.

PAMELA WYNNE

Many knitwear designers wear several hats, but Pamela might deserve the award for wearing the most diverse selection with aplomb. A bona fide rockstar, she spends the summers touring with her band Empty Orchestra, for which she plays keyboard. During the school year, she's an academic, focusing on feminism, politics and culture. Of course, she also finds time to design gorgeous patterns, including collections with Juniper Moon Farm. Pam's blog posts often bring together her various interests and recently she's been continuing that in a series of talks entitled "Untangling the Knitting Culture". Those have developed into a book about the political history of knitting in the United States, which, personally, I'm really looking forward to. I can't think of anyone smarter or more ideally suited to ensuring that the subject is finally treated as seriously as it ought to be. Not that Pam is always serious: her sly sense of humour is visible in many of her designs, and she'll always be remembered at Rhinebeck for her rainbow hot pants.

Ravelry: flintknits
www.flintknits.com

'Bring some cash - while many of the vendors do take credit cards, some lovely booths are cash only (and the ATM machine on the festival grounds can run out).'
— *Mary-Heather Cogar*

BRIAR ROSE FIBERS

Briar Rose Fibers specialise in semi-solid and painterly blends of muted jewel tones that make their booth instantly recognizable at any of the many fibre events they attend each year. Working out of an adorable red barn near Grand Rapids, Michigan, Chris has slowly built a true family business over the last decade. Her son, Nate, built their website. Chris' husband drives the yarn truck so that she can knit while they're on the road, helps to set up and take down booths and, at busier events, works the checkout and bags purchases — apparently happy to be referred to as 'Mr Briar Rose.'

Chris' yarn is beautiful, but chatting with her it's immediately clear how much she enjoys being part of the fibre world. It all began with a class on dyeing, which quickly led to dyeing more yarn and fibre than she could knit or spin herself. Chris began slowly, 'doing the local farmers market and then fiber events.' With the crucial encouragement of family, friends and happy customers she started a website and went from, 'doing events out of the back of my Explorer to hauling a large trailer all over the US'.

That trailer full of yarn really does travel all over, Chris, her husband, and various helpers have a packed schedule that comes out close to a different fibre event every other weekend from March to October. Although the internet allows her to reach a wider market Chris enjoys the personal interaction with customers at events, 'that's one thing you can't get online, even though I do get "virtual" hugs from people'.

Selling at festivals also gives Chris a chance to see what becomes of her art when knitters make it their own: 'I really love seeing finished projects and encourage my customers to bring them to shows. I can't tell you how many people do that!' Chris loves to help people choose the perfect yarn for a project and is keen to encourage knitters to ask her questions at events — she describes her customers with palpable enthusiasm: 'I love hearing that a customer is ready to take the next step and make a sweater, blanket or whatever they have never made before ... I get excited for them too!'

Chris is always happy to give advice on colour selection and yarn substitution, but stresses the importance of buying enough to complete a project. Running out of yarn is always stressful, but hand dyed, limited colourways, mean that more might simply not exist — no matter how hard you search Ravelry stashes. However, if a knitter does run into such problems, Chris, not surprisingly, will do her best to help: 'most of the time I can match a yarn colorway, but it isn't always easy as I really "paint" and do smaller batches.' Shopping at a festival can be overwhelming, so Chris suggests pre-planning and bringing along notes or a copy of the pattern to show the dyer. She does, however, acknowledge that part of the fun is in finding a yarn that wasn't on the plan. 'I love seeing people with their arms full of yarn and then they say "I don't know what I'm going to do with it, but I have to have it!"'

Chris enjoys fibre gatherings so much that this autumn, right before Rhinebeck, Briar Rose will be hosting their own smaller event. Unable to run a regular retail store alongside the dyeing, shipping and travelling to events, this 'Yarn in the Barn' open house weekend will give customers a chance to shop in person. There's also a range of classes taught by local instructors that show Chris' deep enthusiasm for all aspects of fibre production — her visitors can learn everything from skirting a fleece to shaping with stitch patterns.

Rhinebeck remains one of their biggest events of the year, and it's a lot of work for every vendor. So that they can enjoy what Chris describes as 'a big party where we can see almost all of our friends' they try to get there a day early to set their tent with time to rest and get ready for the deluge of people who come through the gate. Even when talking about such a busy event Chris is focused on whether her customers are happy: 'It does get crazy and we hope that we serve people well ... We try to do the best we can do in a limited space and limited selling time.' Just in case, if, amid the racks of inky blues, harvest golds, and forest greens, you're unable to find exactly what you're looking for, she stresses that: 'if you can't find all you need in the booth, we can dye up a batch just for you.' Perfect.

> **I really love seeing finished projects and encourage my customers to bring them to shows. I can't tell you how many people do that!**

Pamela Wynne, who designed the rustic but preppy Aunt Fred pullover worked closely with Chris — her Michigan neighbour — to come up with just the right colour. The process began with the decision to work with an undyed base; a background that would allow the subtleties of the dyed colour to fully emerge. The yarn was also an easy choice. Nate's Yarn, named for Chris' son, is a rustic 2-ply with a slightly uneven texture. The yarn is made in the US, with 'a little vegetable matter now and again to serve as a reminder of how gently it's processed.' In stranded colourwork the result is a cohesive fabric with well-blended patterning and a softly textured appearance. What that contrasting dyed colour should be proved a little more difficult, it started as a forest green. A lovely idea but the contrast ended up giving a sportier feel than Pamela intended. The rich gold was Chris' idea and with it she perfectly captured one of the quintessential parts of my own Rhinebeck experiences — soft autumn light filtered through golden leaves.

Apple Cider Donut

by Cecily Glowik MacDonald

I HAVE FOUND THAT THE WEATHER at the New York Sheep and Wool festival in Rhinebeck, NY in October can be very difficult to predict. I always take that into account when designing my 'Rhinebeck' sweater for each year. Apple Cider Donut is shown with four inches of positive ease so that it may be worn over a t-shirt if the weather is on the warmer side, or used as a jacket over another sweater if the weather is chilly. Buttons are placed at the collar and top of the sweater only to allow for ease of movement. Apple Cider Donut is simply worked from the top down in one piece in stockinette stitch. The stitches for the collar are then picked up and worked in a very easy reversible cable and rib pattern; the collar can be worn up or folded over. The sample uses Fisherman 2-ply from Bartlettyarns, a sturdy yarn that knits up beautifully and quickly.

Pattern directions on page 155.

CECILY GLOWIK MACDONALD

As a designer, it's kind of hard to like Cecily. It's bad enough that she's so prolific — astoundingly Apple Cider Donut is her 164th published sweater pattern — but everything she designs is an excellent balance of wearable and interesting to knit. Fortunately, the fact that Cecily's so sweet makes it impossible to hate her for making the rest of us look lazy. Cecily spent several years as an in-house designer for Classic Elite Yarns, and now designs under her own brand, Winged Knits, and for her Portland, Maine neighbours Quince and Co.

Ravelry: cecilyam
www.cecilyam.wordpress.com

BARTLETTYARNS

First left after the bridge. The town of Harmony Maine isn't on the way to anywhere. A general store: windows not yet boarded up, hopeful 'to let' sign on the door. A small café advertising breakfast, closed; this is not a place where the breakfast hour extends so late into the morning. And then we were crossing the river, the town already behind us. Obediently we turned, reassured each other that it made sense for a mill to be beside the river, we must be going the right way.

There are old mill buildings all over New England, and whether they now house lofts, restaurants or collaborative art spaces, the template is the same. The rows of mullioned windows are familiar, but instead of red brick, a turn in the road presented us with rust. Three stories, the grey metal of a battleship, plus a taller rusted tower.

In nineteen thirteen this metal cladding was state of the art. Two years previously the original mill building — Bartlettyarns has been operating on this site since 1821 — was consumed by wild fire. The river that runs alongside originally powered the mill, before it was converted to electricity in the nineteen forties. The wooden structure might be saturated in machine oil, but it still has its protective, rusty skin. The floors are uneven, with occasional holes, but the top floor reassuringly supports a rack of cast iron running from one end to the other: the mule that makes this place so special.

It was the mule that led current owner, Lindsey Rice, to purchase it. Lindsey and his wife Susan met through their involvement in 4-H as teenagers. Lindsey was a sheep shearer and raised Hampshire sheep, Susan knit and sewed.

(continue)

They first visited Bartlettyarns as customers, taking their fibre to the mill to be custom processed into yarn that they sold at farmers' markets. On one such visit operation had stopped because there was no one on site able to fix a problem with the mule. Lindsey offered to take a look at it — twenty minutes later it was back up and running. When, a few years later, Lindsey was called upon again to fix the mule because the owner was away the visit was quickly followed by a question: 'would you like to buy the mill?'

Lindsey's story is one that feels rather familiar, as much as I love knitting, and wool, it's the machinery that drew me to visit the mill. I love all documentaries about how things are made, it doesn't really matter what the product is: toothpaste, clocks, yarn. My father has a collection of vintage cameras, one day he might be surprised to open the back of one and find a loose screw or lever — bits I somehow had left over when I took them apart and tried to put them back together as a child. Fortunately for Bartlettyarns, I resisted the urge to poke around too much or dismantle anything, satisfying myself with far-too-many close ups of cogs and researching the historical development of spinning technology. Appealing as the idea of tinkering with the mule is, I'm fairly sure they'd have been asking me to leave and never return, not to get more involved, as Lindsey did.

While we were visiting, two farmers pulled up, their long trailer packed tightly with raw fleece. 'Wool accepted here', reads the sign on the shed opposite the mill. And accepted it is. Using a rickety handcart from the thirties, and aided by the farmers, a mill-worker unloads it. One bag at a time.

'Wouldn't it be faster to get a forklift?' I ask. 'The floor is so … " He waves his hand like a snake, slithering along the ground. "And once you change that" he shrugs. I look around, at the uneven floors of dirt and wood, the piles of fleece, sunlight filtering through chinks in the walls. He's right.

From here the fibre will be sent south to a scouring mill, then on to a dye house. Dyeing the wool prior to spinning results in beautifully heathered shades when multiple colours are blended together: 'dyed-in-the-wool'. When it returns to Bartlettyarns it will be unloaded on the mill's lowest floor and tumbled through a needled cylinder that shakes dust from the wool. Inside a windowless room with dark walls, into which everyone who has ever worked there has carved their name, the fibre will wait.

Through ducting that connects one woolly chamber to the other, the fibre will be blown upstairs. Tangled fluff fed into the carder will be teased and rolled into a soft blanket that's poured back and forth in a gentle stream, like molten

chocolate. A second round of rollers will card it more finely, until the final blanket can be split into narrow strands, sliver, and wound onto spools.

Across the room, those spools will be loaded onto the mule, the end attached to a bobbin. When turned on, the bobbins will travel across the floor on their carriage, spinning as they go and drawing the sliver out into a fine thread. At the end of the track, a pause. The mule clicks its claws together, in a motion that adjusts the tension on the bobbins to avoid snarls. The carriage runs back home, winding the newly spun yarn onto the bobbins, and the whole process begins again. When the bobbins are full, each a neatly wound cop, they're removed from the mule and piled high in laundry carts.

The mule is still when we visit, but in the cooler hours of the night it breathes in and out, in a motion that mimics a handspinner's movements. Beside it, cogs and other parts lie in greasy piles. Keeping this fussy machinery running requires a sensitivity to its murmurs, there are no error codes, no catalogue of neatly numbered parts. In the corner workshop there are tools not just for screwing parts together but for machining them. A mirror is mounted above the carder, so that the operator can see problems more easily.

By the time the young woman who works downstairs arrives in the morning the yarn is spun, carts full waiting for her. As she demonstrates how she twists the singles into two and three ply yarns she tells us stories of great aunts and cousins who worked in the mill, of the days of second shifts and operators for each individual machine. The heyday bustle is gone, but the pride and passion is not.

> ❝ Keeping this fussy machinery running requires a sensitivity to its murmurs, there are no error codes, no catalogue of neatly numbered parts. ❞

Instituting changes is a delicate balance. We're shown a process that seems pointless: winding yarn from one type of bobbin to another. But, they tried to make things more efficient and load the bobbins from the mule directly onto the twister. It did not go well. The extra step proved essential for the singles to unwind smoothly and perfectly tensioned.

By the time we've toured the mill, the fibre has been unloaded into the shed. Bags as tall as I am are stacked

(continue)

upright, each tagged with the name of a breed. The farmers belong to the Maine sheep breeders association, and talk enthusiastically about the characteristics of both the fibre and meat from the various breeds. We talk about my recent visit to Nash Island (page 18), and the variety of breeds raised in the state. I'm excited, as always, about breed specific yarns but know that, although Bartlettyarns often spin custom yarns for other companies, that their own yarn line is all local, but blended fibre. There are, certainly, advantages to this, it means they can support more local farmers — many flocks (like the island sheep) are composed of several breeds, interbred over the generations.

> ❝ The floors might be uneven, the tower rusted, the machines aged, but even here they're marketing and producing things that would never have been possible without the Internet and social media. ❞

Before we leave, I ask how they pack the fibre for its journey to be scoured and dyed. The demonstration involves climbing up to the loft, where an empty bag is hooked over a hole in the floor. Packing the fibre tightly involves jumping, literally, on top of it. The balance is tricky, too early and you end up stuck too low, too late and the fibre won't be packed tightly enough. It's a funny sight, but effective. The magic of this place, and the yarn produced here, is as intertwined with the hands (and feet) involved, with the lack of technological upgrades, as the singles run through the twisting machine.

The Fisherman 2-ply that Cecily used for Cider Donut is a classic, rustic woollen spun that's been a staple of Bartlettyarns for more than a century. The same heathered singles are also used to create a bulkier, rounder 3-ply while finer singles are spun for a sport weight that's similar to classic Shetland yarns

and just as ideal for stranded colourwork. For many of Bartlettyarns's loyal customers there's certainly an element of nostalgia involved, indeed one of my companions on the visit, Mary Jane Mucklestone, couldn't resist purchasing an armful because it reminded her of all the knitting she did with it when her children were small. At the same time new customers are finding that Bartlettyarns has been quietly producing the kind of yarns — minimally processed, domestically produced, small-scale, subtle colours — that have seen a resurgence in popularity recently, all along.

Classics might be what Bartlettyarns does well, but that doesn't mean they're out of touch. Recently they were involved in one of the most innovative yarn making projects I've seen — Clara Parkes' Great White Bale. Part education project, part adventure, part yarn club this year long project gave knitters the chance to follow a single bale of fibre as Clara had it processed spun and dyed in batches by some of the most interesting yarn producers in the United States. Subscribers had the option to receive sample skeins of each yarn, and for those who missed out when that sold out quickly there was also an 'armchair traveller' option — a fascinating chance to see the behind the scenes. The first batch of yarn from this project was spun by Bartlettyarns and accompanied by a hilarious video. Posted on the wall of the mill is a list of the equipment, and its date of manufacture: the mule itself is positively new-fangled, at 1948, relative to the 'small card' made in 1882. The floors might be uneven, the tower rusted, the machines aged, but even here they're marketing and producing things that would never have been possible without the Internet and social media.

As we say goodbye to the farmers, to the mill workers, to the women who handle mail-order yarn sales in the office and store, one of whom has been working here for seventeen years, we all agree that we want the story of Bartlettyarns to continue.

·

'The apple cider donuts at the 4-H barn are delicious and served by youth so incredibly polite and cheerful, they will make you feel good about the future of the planet. Definitely a "must have" treat for me every year!'

— *Mary-Heather Cogar*

Mulberry Street

by Melissa Wehrle

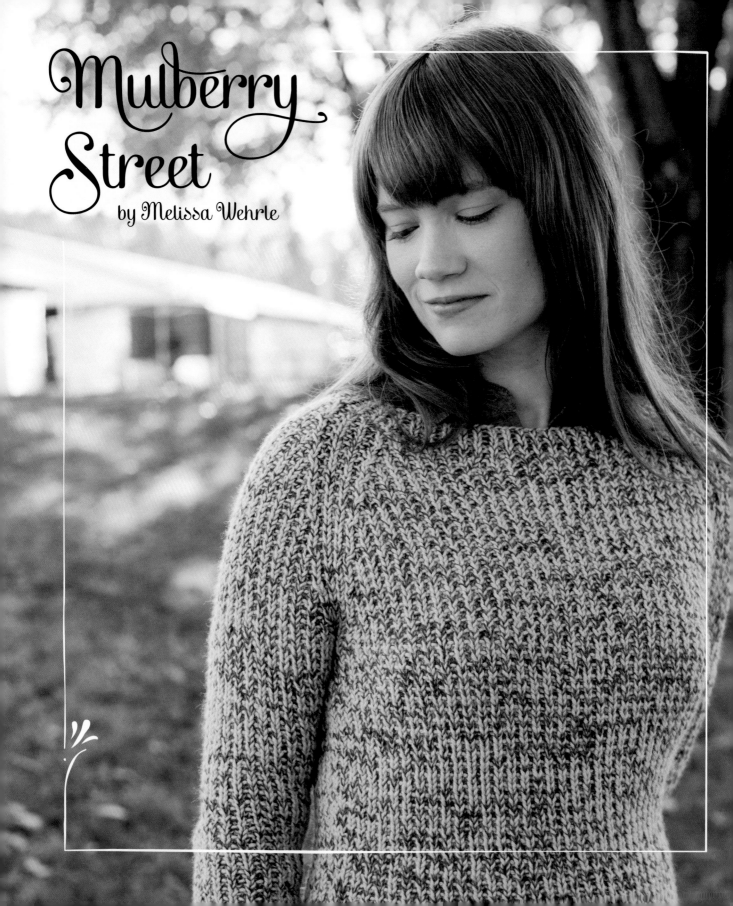

A DECEPTIVELY SIMPLE RAGLAN SWEATER that will be well-noticed on the fairground coming and going. A cute cut-out detail at the upper back brings a little bit of attitude to this marled pullover. Knit all in one piece in a textured stitch using two yarns held together, Mulberry Street makes a great layering piece over a blouse or tee.

Pattern directions on page 160.

Melissa

MELISSA WEHRLE

You might have one of Melissa's sweaters tucked in a drawer without ever realizing it. Not only does she create hand knitting patterns, but she also has a 'real' design job. She learned to knit as a child but her interest in hand knitting was reignited while studying fashion design, with a specialism in knitwear, at the Fashion Institute of Technology in New York City. Melissa currently works as a Senior Designer for a company specialising in juniors' sweaters. Although her day job doesn't involve any hands-on knitting, and often involves more constraints on what can be done because of technological or economic limitations, both of her careers inform each other. Melissa's patterns make excellent use of techniques that are much easier to do by hand — overlapping edges, elaborate stitch patterns, seamless joins — but always show her comprehensive understanding of apparel design. With her glamorous fashion district career and natural model looks I was a little intimidated when I first met Melissa When she sweetly admitted that she'd been afraid to ride the subway when she moved to the city, I was secretly thrilled to discover that she was so normal.

Ravelry: neoknits
www.neoknits.com

THE VERDANT GRYPHON

The first time I met Gryphon Corpus of the Verdant Gryphon (formerly one half of the Sanguine Gryphon) was at an event in a convention centre in the suburbs of Atlanta. Under fluorescent lights, on a concrete floor, in a giant building surrounded by strip malls, they'd created a booth that felt like stepping into another world — I half-expected to walk back out into a fantasy bazaar. Gryphon herself is always bedecked in her 'fanciest gowns', instantly recognisable and wonderfully fun to visit. Somehow, within moments of entering the booth, I found myself being lifted into the air. I'd complained that my feet hurt after standing on the hard floor for hours, and since they didn't have a chair, Gryphon and her colleague Noelle made one for me with their arms.

At Rhinebeck, things can get a little more frenzied, but Gryphon's glowing colourways on well thought out luxury bases are an excellent reward for patience. Try to think of the queue as an opportunity to knit a few rows, and a perfect place to meet other knitters with similar taste. It's been a while since I've had a chance to do more than wave to Gryphon across a crowded marketplace, so it was lovely to take the time to chat with her about her work.

How did you get started?

I launched the business very slowly, around the time my daughter was born, when I knew I didn't want to go back to working for anyone else. I dyed a few skeins of yarn, sold them on Etsy, dyed a few more … and next thing I knew I had a

(continue)

booming business with six people working in my house, and it was time to upgrade to an industrial space.

How has your business changed over the years? What has been the hardest aspect?

Almost everything has changed. When I started, my process was very slow and undeveloped, I had no set procedures for doing anything, and my recipes read something like, 'red, dark blue, a touch of orange' — totally unrepeatable. Over the years, and with the addition of staff, processes have become more sophisticated and efficient: terminology has been developed; systems of recording have been introduced. I think the me of six years ago would be completely boggled by what we have now.

The hardest thing was recognising what the appropriate size is for the business, and having to downsize and restructure the company when it got too big too fast. That was really painful, but I learned many lessons in the process and have a much more stable business now as a result.

That seems to be something a lot of creative people struggle with: at what point does success mean that you're no longer doing the stuff you loved in the first place? How big is your team now, and do you take on extra help for events like Rhinebeck?

Currently I have a fabulous permanent staff of four dedicated people without whom I couldn't get by. This core group gets supplemented in a variety of creative ways, such as part time help from disabled people in our community, administrative temps, and a myriad of wonderful customers helping out with all sorts of things.

What aspects of the yarn making process are you involved in? What do you look for when choosing a new base yarn?

I still keep my hands in most of the steps at least to some extent, though I no longer do much of the production myself. I design the yarn bases myself, in a lengthy back and forth with our mills. I select the fibers, tell the mill what I'm looking for: weight, number of plies, twists per inch, etc. They send me samples, I inevitably say it needs

to be half a twist per inch tighter, or perhaps adjust the fiber content. And so on back and forth until we have something that's perfect.

Once the yarn is in the studio, I develop most of the colourways, though my staff also gets plenty of time to play in the pots and create colours when they are inspired to do so. I do some of the production dyeing, but the great majority is handled by elves Steve the Machine and Leigh Anne the Gardener.

While Leigh Anne is officially in charge of our hanking and tagging department, we all like to step in there now and then and just spend some quiet time handling the yarn, lovingly twisting up each skein, and getting to admire its colours. Sometimes I come in on a Sunday just to listen to a recorded book and hank yarn for hours. It's really therapeutic.

I love that: no matter how much time you spend with yarn it still retains that soothing quality. Can you tell me a bit about your dyeing process and how you develop new colourways (without giving away all of your trade secrets of course!)? Do you think about what people will make with your yarn while you're creating it?

I have a couple different approaches when I set out to create a new colourway. Sometimes I simply have colour inspirations that strike me, combinations that I want to see. At other times I like to work from images. This latter approach is a challenge I've come to enjoy more and more over the years. First, I spend some time just staring at the image, picking out the dominant shades, analysing them, and thinking about which dyes are close or could be mixed to achieve them. Then I have to think about which shades in the image will come about as a result of mixing of the other colours, so that they don't need to be added. For instance, an image from which I recently worked contained brilliant pink, bright blue, deeper blues, and purples. I knew that the pinks and blues I chose would mix to make the darker blues and the purples, so I didn't need to add those dyes separately. Finally, I need to consider how the other shades I'm going to add might throw off ones that

(continue)

I've put in already. In the previous example, when I first mixed the pink it was just right, but when the blue and darker pinks started to go on, they changed the original pink. So I had to go back and rework the first pink such that the shade I wanted would be achieved after the others went on top. It can get quite complicated sometimes!

> " My favourite effects on yarn are the subtle mingling of tones, moody shifts of a thousand shades that are impossible to pin down, so that every stitch might bring a surprise to the knitter. "

What makes your yarn unique?

I think our yarns are unique precisely because of the things I mentioned before — that I design them (often with a great deal of fussiness), and because of the way I think about colour. My favourite effects on yarn are the subtle mingling of tones, moody shifts of a thousand shades that are impossible to pin down, so that every stitch might bring a surprise to the knitter.

Yes! I think the way that Melissa held two colours together really shows off their subtlety. It's a quieter approach than I often see taken with your yarn, but I think it works just as well as something bolder.

These are colours I prefer to knit in sunlight, so that I never miss the action. And of course I'm very particular that our yarns are made only of the highest quality fiber, superb to the touch, spun tightly enough that they won't split, but not to the point of hardness, and giving crisp stitch definition. My aim is always to offer the ultimate luxury yarn.

Do you have any advice for knitters about working with or shopping for hand dyed yarns like yours? What questions should they ask the dyer if they want to know more about the yarn and the kinds of projects it would be ideal for?

One tricky thing about hand dyed yarns, if you can't find project pictures, is knowing how it's going to knit up. When I'm selecting yarn from a dyer whose work I don't know, I look at how the colours are distributed in the skein. If I see larger blocks of colour all together in various parts of the hank I can be pretty sure it's going to stripe or pool. If I see small flecks of colour and many intermediate shades, I can guess that it will give me more subtle distribution. Of course that's harder if it's been re-skeined, but you can still see if there are long strands of a single colour, or if it changes pretty often.

Oh yes, I'm always going back and forth on whether I prefer hand dyed yarns to have been re-skeined. They often look prettier, but it can be more difficult to know how it will behave.

Another thing to look for is the range of darks and lights. If that range is quite wide then I know the yarn will be fairly busy and ill suited to complex stitch patterns. In terms of yarn structure, I look for a tight ply and crisp outer appearance to the yarn, which I know will mean better stitch definition, stronger wear, and less likelihood of pilling.

You seem to focus more on selling online than wholesale or in person sales, why did you decide to focus your business in that way?

I love selling in person, but we're based in a small town, which I do not think could sustain us, given our small, specialised product range. The internet provides us a much larger audience. As to wholesale, while it is certainly easier in some regards, I especially value the direct feedback we're able to get by retailing directly. If we dye a colour and it sells out very quickly, we can hear immediately from our customers that they want more, and provide it right away.

What about the community aspect of shows and festivals, firstly is that important to your business, but also do you enjoy being part of that? Does it fulfill something that the internet cannot, however great Ravelry is?

The shows are simply wonderful and I love everything about them (except maybe how exhausted I am afterwards). It's great to meet our customers in person. We chat with some of these people all the time on Ravelry, they become our friends, but we hardly ever get to meet them. Shows are often the only time that changes,

> ❝ As far as I'm concerned, a fiber festival is a party and I like to celebrate in high style! ❞

and we get to see their smiling faces in person. Moreover, shows are of course a fantastic way to introduce our yarn to new people. Many wander by who have never heard of us before and fall in love with the yarn in the booth; others have seen our yarn online but were leery of buying until they could meet it in person. And then of course there's the delightful sociable aspect of it, getting to spend an entire weekend in the company of fellow yarn-lovers, simply hanging out and chatting. Finally, I personally get really into the theatrical aspect of it. I like to deck out our booth festively, pull out my fanciest gowns for the occasion, play music, and sometimes even do a bit of belly dancing during a quiet patch. As far as I'm concerned, a fiber festival is a party and I like to celebrate in high style!

What is being a vendor at a festival like Rhinebeck like? I'm sure it's a ton of work, but can you give us any behind-the-scenes insight?

Rhinebeck is one of the ultimate fiber festivals, packed with people and brilliant colours and adorable animals and delicious smells. While the actual booth work is fun, I also love other parts of the show time. On set-up day I always make time to sneak away for a while and

wander around the animal barns, for this is the day the farmers are busiest. Sheep are being walked to and from pens, getting the finishing touches put on their coiffures, and all is a joyful riot of baaing and bleating. Another aspect which festival-goers may not see is the camaraderie among the vendors. At every show there is a host of familiar faces, many of them ones I see only at shows. We help each other out, share tools, watch each other's booths for bathroom breaks, etc. I always make sure to make my rounds and say hello to all my old vendor friends, and maybe make a few new ones. And I've hatched more than a few madcap ideas and collaborations while visiting someone's booth: "Hey, what if we … ?"

I know those conversations all too well, that's how I ended up doing this project in the first place!

•

Artichoke French

by Laura Nelkin

MANY YEARS, going to Rhinebeck can be a chilly adventure. I've found that what I really like is not to be encumbered by too many layers and accessories. Simplicity is the key to having a great time! So, having a thick warm sweater that is well fitted AND has integrated fingerless mitts is rather perfect … I can wear less AND be warm! It means I don't have to take off my mittens to eat my way through the festival or knit while I catch up with old friends.

Artichoke French is worked seamlessly, from the bottom up, in the round with raglan shaping and a mock turtleneck. Thumbholes are integrated into the elongated sleeves; if you want to skip this AWESOME design element, just cast on for the sleeves right after the thumbhole is worked.

Pattern directions on page 165.

LAURA'S HOMEMADE ARTICHOKE FRENCH

This version is a wee bit different than available at Rhinebeck … the artichoke flavor is stronger, and I introduced some wine, because I felt like it. If you want it as part of a whole meal consider putting it on top of a pile of beans and greens.

Ingredients

1 can whole artichoke hearts (approx. 14 oz / 400g before draining)

1 cup / 150g all-purpose / plain flour

salt and pepper to taste

2 large eggs

1 tablespoon / 15ml lemon juice

3 tablespoons / 45g butter

2 tablespoon / 30ml olive oil

1 cup / 150ml lovely white wine (use a wine you would want to drink)

1oz / 25g Parmesan cheese, finely grated

1 tablespoon fresh parsley, chopped

hot pepper or hot sauce (optional)

Directions

Prepare the artichokes and batter: drain the artichokes well, and slice in half. In a shallow bowl mix the flour with salt and pepper. In a separate shallow bowl beat together the eggs and lemon juice.

Coat artichokes in batter: dip each artichoke in the flour mixture, shake of excess; then dip in the egg mixture taking care to coat both sides thoroughly; place back into the flour mixture coating on both sides again.

Fry the hearts: heat the olive oil in a heavy frying pan over medium heat. When a small amount of flour dropped in pan sizzles and browns add the artichokes (cook in batches if necessary). When they are browned on one side flip over and squash with the backside of your spatula. When browned on both sides remove from pan and drain oil on a few layers of paper towel.

Make the sauce: add the wine and butter to the pan and continue cooking until reduced and thickened. There should be enough excess flour from the hearts in the pan for the sauce to thicken but if necessary stir in a spoonful of the leftover flour mixture.

Serving: place artichokes in serving dish and top with sauce, then garnish with liberal amounts of grated Parmesan and parsley. If you are a hot pepper or hot sauce lover (like I am) add to your dish before eating!

LAURA NELKIN

Since leaving her stint as Design director of Schaefer Yarn Company to branch out on her own, Laura has carved out a successful niche as an independent designer. Her work is focused primarily on beaded accessories that she packages as kits with well-curated combinations of beads and hand-dyed yarns. However, as Artichoke French shows, her sweater design skills are just as well honed. Laura has a mischievous grin, and she almost got me in trouble with Jill Draper, whose yarn she used. Throughout all of our discussions about yarn, Laura referred to it as 'big balls' — I never questioned that, and it wasn't until I talked to Jill herself that I found out the yarn's real name is 'Empire'. Jill was horrified, but I still think it would have been funny if we'd printed it as 'Jill Draper's big balls'. And now she'll probably kill me, since I'm telling you the story.

Ravelry name: lauranelkin
Website: www.nelkindesigns.com

JILL DRAPER MAKES STUFF

I find it impossible to imagine Jill except through a haze of vibrantly coloured wool — surrounded by the full spectrum of the rainbow in skein form, pulling off the most surprising clothing combinations perfectly, laughing. Her enthusiasm for this craft, combining wool and colour, is infectious, and she's keen to share her success — seeking out passionate small producers to work with. She loved the New York Sheep and Wool Festival so much that she moved to the area. To all appearances, Jill has found her thing.

It might be surprising then, to discover that Jill Draper started dyeing yarn on a whim. She was living in New York City, studying fashion at Pratt Institute. Unable to find the perfect yarn to use in a knitwear collection, dyeing her own seemed like a logical solution. She began, like many dyers, in the kitchen sink. That first handful of yarn for her collection had her hooked.

Jill fell in love with being able to manipulate the medium, starting one step further back in the process of creating a garment, working with the raw material — being able to 'control the way the colours landed'. Ever since, Jill has continued to work her way backwards, working directly with farmers and mills to involve herself in all aspects of the production process. It's an expansive approach; creating patterns allows Jill to remain involved with the design end.

Moving upstate was motivated partly by a desire to be closer to the rich craft community she'd discovered in the Hudson Valley, but being able to afford more space was also compelling: 'when I left Brooklyn I realized I could probably do this full time … I expanded the business and started buying more undyed commercial bases to dye.' Quickly, however, working with existing bases became constraining: 'I wanted to have more control over the bases that were available; I wanted things that weren't the same bases that everyone else was using. When I first started dyeing from commercial bases it seemed like the only kinds of wool that were available were Merino and some generic unlabeled wool.'

And so, she found herself visiting a mill. Stacked up outside were giant bags, overflowing with all kinds of fleece: 'it was like the first time you go to a farmer's market and realize there are "kinds" of tomatoes or that apples aren't just green or red. I wanted to stick my hands and face into every bag, pull out little tufts of wool, examine & compare them in the light.' It quickly became clear what was missing in the commercial bases she'd previously been using and Jill set out to have her own milled; yarns 'that really took advantage of the different characteristics of each fibre and showed it to its best effect.'

The result is a unique range of hand dyed yarns. One of which, Artemis a 2-ply mohair and Romney lambswool blend, includes fibre that's especially close to home, 'the mohair is from my mom's goats. She only has a tiny flock, it's really a hobby, but those goats make some incredibly beautiful mohair fibre that we blend with Romney from a local farm.'

Empire, the yarn Laura used for Artichoke French, is made from Rambouillet, one of the fibres Jill initially encountered on that visit, 'one of the wools I was most attracted to was a bag labeled Rambouillet. I had never heard of this breed before but loved the fine, crimped, greasy, lock of wool I held in my hand. The mill connected me with the farmer who raises the Rambouillet whose wool filled that bag. Tom, on his farm in Albany County raises Rambouillet sheep, honey bees and, off-site, peonies. He is tall, tan, mustachioed, has a super quick smile and friendly way about him. He takes a great amount of pride in the wool he produces and he has reason to. Rambouillet is medium-fine wool, a dual-purpose breed that had its start in Europe but is thriving now in the US.

The sheep are large, comparative to other breeds, strong and free from the skin folds that can be problematic for their Merino "cousins". The staple is around 3 – 4" and although somewhat greasy, is much less so than Merino fleece generally is.'

'I knew this wool wanted to be "sweater" yarn, the kind of yarn that is soft enough to wear next to your skin but hearty enough you can actually do outside chores without the worry of ruining a precious knit and will still look good after years of hard wear. I decided a highly twisted 4-ply yarn was the way to go to give a little added strength and springiness to these fine fibers. Aran weight seemed like a natural fit; after all I'm an Upstate New Yorker and we spend a lot of time outside and in sweaters. The yarn is made for me at the wonderful Green Mountain Spinnery in Vermont' —one of several mills Jill now works with to create different types of yarn — 'where it is washed without the use of petroleum by-products and put up into gigantic hanks of 1280 yards, weighing in at almost 2 pounds. I've had to expand from only using Tom's flock, although they are still part of the line, the demand for Empire has grown beyond their output so Rambouillet from the Western US is also included. My yearly visits to Tom's farm are still one of the highlights of my early Summer, and not just for the honey, kitten snuggles and peonies, although those are pretty great bonuses.'

Jill is passionate not just about working with breeds beyond Merino but about introducing knitters to breeds they might not have encountered before. She's excited to tell me about the unusual crimp pattern of the Cheviot used in her yarn, Valkill, 'It has a helical crimp. Most sheeps' wool is crimped as if you had a crimping iron on your hair but Cheviot is crimped in three dimensions so it gives a really hardwearing and resilient fibre but I still think it's soft enough to wear next to your skin. I have it plied in a similar twist to the Icelandic Lopi yarns.'

At the heart of Jill's business is the desire to create yarns: 'that have as small and as ethical of a footprint as possible.' She's slowly been bringing her line closer to home, and recently announced that all of her future yarns will be

(continue)

entirely grown and processed in the United States. Even when she worked with mills further afield she sought out ones in Japan, although there were countries where: 'I could have them milled much less expensively but it was important to me that there were certain work standards and environmental standards.'

66 *I think the love that goes into the yarn sort of transfers into the project.* 99

Such ethical standards also affect the quality of the yarn, in both a literal and figurative sense. The mill that spins Mohonk avoids petroleum based washes, which has obvious environmental benefits but also means that the yarn 'retains some of its natural lanolin, which I think makes it really nice to knit and to wear. It's so soft and squishy.' Jill's smile is wry as she tells me 'I think the love that goes into the yarn sort of transfers into the project.' She blushes, 'That sounds kind of hippyish.' It does, but is there any other way to say this? If knitters didn't recognize the truth of this rather fuzzy concept, would we care so much about giving hand knits to show our love?

Jill is eager to see the increased interest in where food comes from extending to other areas, including clothing and fibre production. 'I think that it matters in all aspects of our lives. I think where you buy your clothes from, what yarn you knit with, I think it's all aspects of living a conscientious life.' This isn't a hobby, or solely a creative pursuit: creating a viable business, one that helps other small businesses to thrive, is a mission Jill takes seriously. She's one the most professional businesswomen I know, working with a wide range of other companies, balancing customer service, dyeing, designing and selling at events.

As I walked through the marketplace at a recent event, right after the doors closed, I passed understandably flustered vendors trying to pack up at the end of a long weekend, snapping 'this needs to go in the box first', 'where's the tape?' at each other. It was chaos, I've done enough shows myself to know exactly how they felt. And then I got to Jill's booth, planning to quickly say hi before getting out of the way. There was Jill, surrounded by neatly packed, closed tubs, joking with the convention workers: downstairs her boyfriend was waiting with the truck, yes they could take their stuff out so early. As they loaded up her yarn, Jill asked if I was interested in anything. After teaching all weekend, this was the first I'd seen of the marketplace. Well … I appeared to be too late, but I mentioned one of her new yarns. Without hesitation, Jill picked out the exact box, pulled out a skein and proceeded to tell me its story.

· · · · · · ● · · · · · ·

'Bring expandable shopping bags
(like a Chico), and WATER!'
— *Laura Nelkin*

'There's a lot of great food to try so team up with friends so you can taste the widest selection before you're too full — I loved the fried pickles. Sunscreen is a good idea, even though it can be cool it's a long day outdoors.'

— *Rebecca Redston*

Spring Brook

by Connie Chang Chinchio

DESPITE BEING WORKED IN SOCK-WEIGHT YARN, this light vest, framed in a simple lace, is very fast to knit up. The front bands are knit at the same time as the body of the vest and continue around the back neck. Leave the edges raw for a casual look, or single crochet a narrow edging around the armholes and hem for a polished look.

Pattern directions on *page 170.*

Connie

CONNIE CHANG CHINCHIO

I'd never even met Connie when she invited me to stay at her apartment on my first visit to New York City. Fortunately she turned out to be about as far away from a serial killer as you could possibly imagine: Connie's one of the most warm-hearted people I know. Her design work has a certain sweetness too, focusing on classic feminine sweaters with pretty details. The lace and textural motifs that Connie uses fit together with a knitterly precision that hints at her background in physics. When she was heavily pregnant with her first child Connie braved the bitter winds of a New York January to meet me for brunch, she arrived with a full bag of yarn. She'd never crocheted before, but had decided to make a granny square baby blanket. A naturally skilled crafter; it only took me a couple of minutes to show her what to do.

Ravelry: changcon
www.conniechangchinchio.com

BIJOU BASIN

I met Eileen and Carl Koop at the first of these festivals I ever went to, Maryland Sheep and Wool, in 2009. It was the first time I'd met many of the people in this funny world I'd stumbled into by putting a few patterns on the Internet. Although many of them are now dear friends, the owners of Bijou Basin were particularly memorable. Carl is a born storyteller, who, despite the self-deprecating jokes, takes the mission of creating uniquely beautiful luxury yarns extremely seriously.

I don't know if it's simply because they're both so tall (although admittedly everyone over 5' 6" is tall from my point of view), or a personality thing, but it's always seemed perfectly natural that the couple raised Irish Wolfhounds — and now yaks — at their home in Colorado. However, that hasn't always been the case: their former careers were very different. Carl was a software developer and Eileen, head of research and development for OxiClean. Nor were they passionate knitters or spinners eager to develop a hobby into a career. It's become a bit of a running joke — which he is good humoured enough to tolerate — that I offer to teach Carl to knit every time I see him. (I'll get him one day.)

So, when I had the chance to sit down with Carl at a recent trade show (got to love someone who includes a couch in their booth display) I was eager to find out how they'd ended up with not just a yarn company, but a yak yarn company.

How on earth did you get involved in farming yaks?

I did software development for about 30 years but got tired of it. I quit my job, went to school, got a 3 year degree in animal science and got myself certified as a veterinary technician. I started working for a large animal veterinarian. I was out on a ranch call vaccinating horses and two little yaks came walking out of the barn. I asked the woman who owned them: 'What the hell am I looking at? I just got out of school and I didn't sleep through that many classes.'

Eileen and I had been looking to find an agriculture business to keep our agriculture tax status, and as something we could retire into. Which is a whole 'nother story. I've never worked so hard in my life. But the little yaks just attracted me and literally bit me on the butt at one point.

We decided to get a couple of yaks, put them on the ranch. So I looked around and found some folks were doing yak fibre on a real true mom and pop level. While we're just barely above that, we did it a little bit more sophisticated. Most people would comb their yaks, spin it and sell it at a farmers' market. We decided to do a bigger scale operation. We bought fibre from other people as well as our own, and now we actually import fibre from Tibet and Nepal. But it started because I had a couple of little six month old yaks come up and bite me on the butt while I was trying to vaccinate horses.

You don't knit, right? So how do you work with knitters to make sure that your yarns work well?

Most of the blends are done by my wife. Eileen will sit down and figure out which fibres she wants, what's going to work well together. We have a group of knitters; most of them are designers as well. We'll get a sample run from a mill of x number of skeins and we'll distribute those out: let people see them and touch them. The rest of the skeins will go to a dye house — we work with Lorna's Laces — to let them start dyeing and make sure things are going to work the way we want. So we have people who actually know what they're doing help us work with that. If it's a good blend: great. If it's not we'll try and figure out what the complaints are, what the problems are, and we'll adjust the amount of fibre. It's like our Lhasa Wilderness: the yak and bamboo. A lot of people don't like bamboo because

it just hangs; it has no memory. So we tried to keep the amount of bamboo down. It took us two or three shots to get what we think is just the right amount of bamboo.

> 66 But it started because I had a couple of little six month old yaks come up and bite me on the butt while I was trying to vaccinate horses. 99

What makes the yak fibre unique?

Yak fibre is a true wool: it's got crimp, it's got scale, it's a solid fibre. Yak fibre is three to five times warmer than most of the average sheep's wool. It's more breathable than sheep's wool, so you don't feel all hot and sweaty when you're wearing it. So the plus side is that you don't have to wear a big heavy garment; you can wear something that's lightweight. It will be very warm and as you go indoors and outdoors you don't have to worry about taking it off all the time because it's so breathable. Because it's a true wool, it has memory. That's another unique thing within the high end exotic fibres. Most of them don't have memory because they're hairs, like musk ox and bison. They're a hollow fibre. Yak does have memory to it. So when we add it to silk, bamboo, things like that, you get all the properties of those fibres plus the property of the yak which brings in memory. Like I was saying, with the Lhasa Wilderness you have that drape from the bamboo but you have memory, so you have a garment that will stretch and will move with you. And it's incredibly soft. Right in the mid range, 16 to 19 microns, which puts us right in the middle of cashmere.

The yarn Connie chose for her vest, Tibetan Dream, is a blend of yak and nylon, described as a sock yarn. Can you tell me a little more about that yarn? How do you decide whether a particular yarn will work best with a blend of fibres? It seems like you're considering the kinds of projects it might be used for throughout the process?

(continue)

Tibetan Dream was originally meant to be our sock yarn. Yak fibre makes great socks: it's nice and toasty warm but your feet don't get all sweaty from it. The best part of it is it will wear forever, even though it's incredibly soft it will wear forever. The drawback to yak fibre is that it's a very short fibre: the staple length is only ¾", maybe on a good day 1¼", and what will happen is along the sole of the foot there's a lot of lateral tension there. The fibres don't wear out but if you used 100 per cent yak they'd start to pull apart. So you need a long fibre in there to maintain that lateral strength. So we went with a nylon. Very specifically, my wife, the chemist, decided to use a nylon with a diameter finer than the yak fibre. We only used 15 per cent, which is just enough to get us that extra strength. So it's 85 per cent yak fibre, and since the yak fibre is thicker than the nylon, what you're feeling is 99 per cent yak fibre. But I also think that eight out of ten skeins don't become socks. People use it for all sorts of things.

This yarn was hand dyed by Lorna's Laces: can you tell me a bit more about that collaboration?

For a long time all we carried was the natural browns and creams. A lot of people wanted us to start dyeing. We said, we have a nice high end product we want a good quality dye house to work with. While there are tons of dyers around, they either need thousands of pounds to come in, or they can only handle a few pounds occasionally — *scaling is such a common problem in this industry!* — So we had a short list of half a dozen people we wanted to talk to. We were at a trade show — it happened to be the TNNA show — and Beth Casey from Lorna's Laces came over to chat about the show. As she was leaving she said, 'Oh hey guys, by the way if you ever want me to dye your fibre let me know, give me a yell.' And I said, fine. She was on our short list; she was high up on our list. — *he grins* — So I let her get about twenty feet away before I yelled at her, because she said 'give me a yell'. That was at a January show, and by the June show of the same year we had hoped to have one blend of our yarn dyed in six colours. They were so hard to deal with — *the grin appears again* — we ended up with three blends of our yarn being dyed, and in thirteen colours.

Tell me a bit about your yaks. When I visited the ranch I was struck by how much personality they have and how well you know them all.

In Colorado we're in the fourth year of a real bad drought, so I've had to sell off a lot of my animals because the pasture can't sustain as many animals and hay prices are through the roof. So unless I want to pass that along to the consumer, my option was to decrease my herd a little bit. But it is important to us to have our animals and when the drought releases we're going to go ahead and build our herd back up. We hand raise our animals, not bottle feed, but they're accustomed to us, they respect us, it's ok for us to be in the middle of the herd.

They like that, they like to interact with us but they also understand that we're not yaks. The importance of that is that if they think you're a yak they'll play with you like a yak. In the case of some of our steers that's a twelve hundred pound somebody saying 'hey, let's butt heads,' because that's what they do for fun. And you're not going to win that fight. So we do want them to understand that differentiation. We also have a lot of people who come out and visit the ranch, strangers. So my animals have gotten to the point where when they see a stranger coming, they come to the fence because it means free treats. They all have names, they're all part of the family. In the spring we comb the fibre from our animals. That's part of the process for us; it always has been and always will be.

You can see personality for each animal within a day or two of when they are born. The little boys are always buttheads. They get to a certain point and they literally just start butting heads with everything they can, trying to see if they can beat it up. But you'll see that some of them are much more outgoing, some of them are more curious. Others are a little shy and will stay off in the background a little bit. It's actually pretty funny to watch them grow.

Has there been a learning curve to becoming farmers? Have you had any problems along the way?

My wife and I, other than my veterinary training, didn't have any experience with large animals so everything's

(continue)

'I recommend setting aside some time to see the animals in the barns, and I always love to watch the Sheep Dog Herding Demonstrations. Seeing the hardworking dogs and getting a glimpse of farm life is a really special opportunity - not to mention, really fun for a herding dog lover like myself!'

— *Mary-Heather Cogar*

gone wrong at some point. But it's all been fun; it's all been a learning experience. We really do enjoy it; we have a good time with the animals. It's usually when we try and do something new with the animals that something happens.

We had Sherman. When Sherman was born his mother retained part of her placenta. She wasn't feeling good for a day or two. They didn't bond as well as they could have. We would have to pick Sherman up and put him under her so he would nurse. She was fine when we did that but she wouldn't grunt and call him over, remind him. As a result Sherman's response to being touched by humans was to go limp. So as Sherman got older and was six hundred pounds you could walk over to him and scratch him real hard on the sides. He liked it but all of a sudden you'd see his legs get wobbly and he'd fall over. I always threatened to take him into town for a bar bet: say 'I bet you a dollar I can knock this yak over with one hand.'

> ❝ *If I could figure out how to get you to touch the fibre in an email I'd be in much better shape.* ❞

There are lots of goofy stories like that but we've never really had any major issues. They're very healthy animals, they're pretty disease resistant so that's been working out good. — *it makes a big difference that their ranch is located in Colorado, at a similar high altitude to the yak's native Tibet —* It's the looks you get from the veterinarian the first time he shows up. You don't tell the veterinarian that he's coming out to look at yaks. You say 'I know you do cattle so you'll come out and look at mine, right?' And when he gets there: 'oh look at that, they're actually yaks.'

You always seem to be on the road, going to different festivals! Do you think the fact that your yarn is so unique, and that it's a luxury fibre, means that people really need to see it in person to understand it?

There's a couple of things that we get from doing that one-on-one with the consumer. First of all, we've made a lot of really good friends. There's a lot of people who come to the same shows over and over and we've gotten to the point where we look forward to seeing them. The other thing that I really like is that we get to see the reaction to the colours, to the yarn blend. We get to talk to the consumer and see what it is that they like and don't like. If I did that through a shop owner, I'd be getting their interpretation of what the consumer may have told them. And the consumer may not have been totally honest with them, but when they know they're dealing with the ranchers they're painfully frank with us. It works out well that way because sometimes people say 'oh it's the price' or 'I'm allergic to wool so I can't wear this'. So we get to work with people and show them what's going on.

The other thing is that everybody has an uncle, or a cousin, or a friend of a friend who has been to Tibet. I'm stunned that that many people in the world have been to such a small country. But most of them have brought back a ball of yarn or something and people come in and say 'yak fibre? Oh my god, that's horrible: itchy and scratchy'. And the stuff that comes from Tibet is, because their use of the fibre is completely different from ours. So it's great to be able to draw people into the booth. The thing I say to a lot of people is: 'you gotta come in and touch it, I'm not going to make you buy it but you do have to touch it so you know what the difference is between this and what uncle Phil brought home from Kathmandu.' 100 per cent yak fibre is an incredibly soft yarn and people are stunned. In the booth we usually have pictures of the animals from the ranch. They stand there and they look and they say 'this yarn, this softness came from those animals?' So that's a lot of fun to really introduce people to the fibre. If I could figure out how to get you to touch the fibre in an email I'd be in much better shape.

What is being a vendor at a festival like Rhinebeck like? I'm sure it's a ton of work, but can you give us any behind-the-scenes insight?

What people don't realize is, people come into the show, they show up at 9 o'clock when the show opens and expect everything to be going smooth and that's what we want. Everything that's in the booth — tables, garment rails, tablecloths, the yarn — has to be packed up at our house into bins and boxes. Then we drive it up to a shipper who puts it on pallets and shrink-wraps it. We arrive two days before a show and get everything ready, so we can make it look seamless to people. When they leave we start the process in the opposite direction. My wife, thank goodness, does all of the logistics. Last fall we did six shows in four weeks. That meant we had three shows' worth of pallets flying around the country to different sites. When we got to the show we hoped everything was there: knock on wood we've not had a problem with that. I don't think people realize how much work goes in beforehand. And then from 9am to 6 in the evening we're on talking to people. We love doing that but by the end of the day, oh my god you're exhausted.

Rhinebeck has been a show that we absolutely love to do; it's one of our favourite shows. The folks at Rhinebeck, the people who work the show, have been very, very good to us and we appreciate that. More importantly, and I think this sounds strange to people who haven't been there, but New York state is a great place to be in the autumn. The weather's usually good; you've got those crisp days with the bright blue sky, the fall colours on all the old hardwood trees. Rhinebeck and all the sheep and wools we do, those are my favourite shows. There's a different feel to those shows. The shows that are in convention centres are great shows and we love doing them, but when you're outdoors, in a tent or in a building that's got all the doors open, it's just a much better feeling and I really love that.

As a kid my father used to take us to the county fair. It was in a different county because the county I lived in was five miles outside Manhattan — we didn't have a lot of livestock. But we'd go to Northwest New Jersey, to the Morris county fair. I have this odd sense memory, when I smell manure, of going to the county fair and how much fun I had. I'm not talking a feedlot or something like that, I don't want it for cologne, but I have these good sense memories. So when we go to the sheep and wool that's part of it: the noise from the animals, the sheep constantly making their little bleats, and every five minutes or so you'll get a whiff of manure. You've got a great day for the weather, you've got all these friends coming into the booth and I get that sense memory going and I just adore the autumn shows, I really, really do.

We brought two baby yaks to a show in Colorado. The funny part of that is that they weren't my yaks; I borrowed yaks. At that point we were brand new. We had three cows and a bull. I didn't want to bring the bull, that's not a good thing, and the three cows I didn't want to stress out. So I went to a friend that had six-month-old baby yaks and I borrowed them. People loved them. Baby yaks are just cute, there's no two ways about it. The people went nuts over them but it got to the point where they were getting too grabby. So I had to be outside with them, which put a lot more pressure on Eileen to run the booth herself. So since then we've not taken them ourselves, we've had friends bring yaks to different shows. It always does raise eyebrows when people see them. They're very cow like, they are part of the bovine family. But there's just something not right: they've got those big horns and that big hump on their backs.

People should not be afraid to talk to the vendors. Especially at the sheep and wool festivals it can get nuts, it can be hard to get to a vendor. But if you have a real interest in the animals that are providing the fibre, or even just the fibre itself you shouldn't feel bad about annoying the vendors. Sometimes I can't stop and talk to people as much as I'd like to but every show I have people who stand there and wait so they can talk about the yaks. We love to do that and I know most of the other vendors do to. At those kind of shows people aren't just selling products, as distributors. They're selling their products; their heart and soul has gone into what's there. We're all proud of what we've got and we love to take that time. So I don't think people should feel bad about annoying the vendors with questions, we love answering those questions. And be patient, sometimes, there are always breaks in the activity, but there are times when the booth just runs full bore for hours on end. Come over, if we're busy, wander around the show a little more. And make sure you have something to eat, if you're there all day it's a long day. I wish I could get out of the booth more, not necessarily to shop but just to see what else other people have.

They might look kind of absurd, but I think the yaks are adorable, and their fibre is very special.

●

Maple Cotton Candy

by Amy Herzog

MAPLE COTTON CANDY IS MY FAVOURITE KIND OF FESTIVAL SWEATER: subtle, flattering, and able to handle any kind of weather. It layers well, works beautifully with a hand-knit scarf or shawl, and provides the perfect showcase for some truly special buttons.

Maple Cotton Candy is worked in pieces from the bottom up and seamed, with set-in sleeves. The textured stitch beautifully shows off subtly variegated yarn without being too busy or difficult to shape, and the seed stitch makes for a lovely accent.

I used Fiber Optic Superwash Merino Worsted for this sweater, a lovely springy yarn with beautiful stitch definition that I couldn't resist at Rhinebeck in 2010. The buttons are also from a NYS&W vendor named Shipyard Point Glassworks. They're a wonderful glassworks vendor, and I make a point of spending an unreasonable amount of time in their booth every fall.

Pattern directions on page 175.

AMY HERZOG

Perhaps more than anyone else, Amy shares my passion for helping all women achieve a simple, but often elusive goal: sweaters that fit, flatter, and make them feel wonderful. Over the last few years Amy has turned a popular series of blog tutorials, 'Fit to Flatter,' into classes that she teaches all over the United States; and most recently has published a book, Knit to Flatter. She's also a prolific designer, focusing on classic, wearable garments to suit a range of shapes. Her current project is a software program that will help knitters to generate a custom sweater pattern with a perfect fit for their measurements: CustomFit.

Ravelry: amyherzog
www.amyherzogdesigns.com

FIBER OPTIC

Kimber Baldwin was working as a research scientist at The University of Cincinatti in 2006, frustrated that long days in the lab didn't leave enough time for her children. Time at home after the birth of her third child, Emily, was welcome, but Kimber was unprepared for the lack of structure in her days: 'There was simply too much free time!' A knitter for three decades, Kimber's interest in yarn and the interplay of colours led to naptimes spent researching the mechanics of acid dyeing.

Two years later, when her youngest child was born, Kimber once again found herself with free time at home. This time she felt ready to put her research into practice: developing formulas for thousands of colours, from which she created a working palette of her favorites. The business started small, selling a few skeins to friends and on Etsy; a time that Kimber describes as 'creatively vibrant.' This period of quiet growth came to an abrupt end when a customer gave a skein to Stephanie Pearl-McPhee. Many yarnies have experienced 'The Yarn Harlot Effect:' a boost in sales after the popular blogger writes about their products. Stephanie's blog post about knitting a pair of socks not only resulted in a dramatic increase in orders, but it also garnered interest from others in the fibre community. One of those people was Toni Neil, owner of The Fold, who was looking for a dyer interested in selling on consignment at Sock Summit 2009. 'Never having been at a major fiber festival, I thought it sounded like a huge amount of fun! Toni and I hit it off and spent the next year together on the festival circuit — she took me under her wing and mentored me on vending at various fiber festivals.' In 2010 Fiber Optic had their own booth at Rhinebeck for the first time.

Kimber's desire for greater balance between her home and work lives led to starting the business, which she

finds makes it possible 'to eliminate the artificial borders between family and career.' Her children sit in on meetings, play in the materials area, and are growing up knowing yarn weights and fibre staple lengths. 'When Emily was 2 she could identify the breed of sheep in our top (Merino, BFL, Wensleydale) by the smell — I didn't even know this was possible until she pointed out to me that the wools smelled differently.'

What started as a naptime activity has now grown beyond a full time job for Kimber, who currently has several employees. 'Besides myself, there is Denise, our materials handling manager. She oversees everything from receiving yarns and fibers from the mills to sending out dyed yarns and fiber to contractors for braiding, winding, and packaging. Our dye studio manager, Cori, is in charge of the production dyeing. While I do quite a bit of that too, most of my time lately is split between creative colorway development and administrative tasks. Cori takes the dye formulations and protocols and turns them into yarn and fiber. Finally, Ellie does most of the fiber braiding and packaging as well as partnering with me at fiber festivals.'

The scale might have changed but creative curiosity remains the core motivation of the business. 'Our business model embraces the ever-changing nature of the fiber/yarn community. If you can't beat 'em, join 'em. I really crave creativity so Fiber Optic Yarns is about new products, colors, dye applications, set techniques. I can't remember the last time an entire day went by without hearing (or asking) the question, "How can we make this better?" I tell folks that Fiber Optic Yarns is a collaboration of the personal yarn/fiber stashes of the ladies who work here — we have to be excited about it and want to own it more than what is currently available or we don't carry it.'

(continue)

That collaborative approach extends to the process of selecting a new base yarn. They start with a sample of 5 – 10 pounds, and any member of the team has the authority to call a halt: 'everyone brings a different perspective to the table and it's important to take advantage of this since we are selling to a wide audience with a variety of preferences.' They then put the potential base yarn through its paces: 'we dye it, knit it, wash it, block it, and wear it, evaluating it at every step. We knit lace, cables, big items, little accessories — if it falls short in any way, we toss it in the scrap bin (we have a lot of yarn in that bin). It took over two years, and a couple of dozen different base yarns, before we fell in love with the yarn that Amy used for her sweater: a 4-ply spun from a long-staple Merino that is then plied around a very thin core of air. It is spin-balanced and not over twisted, while at the same time it is also dense, smooth, and very elastic. It has everything we wanted in a worsted weight wool — soft, superwash, gives great stitch definition, and holds up well, wash after wash.'

Kimber's science background is immediately evident when she describes their dyeing process, which varies depending on the goal for that yarn: 'We begin with a concept of what we want the skein to look like and how it will knit up — then I go back to the chemical properties of the primary dyes and work up a protocol to achieve the desired color effect. We have completely different protocols, depending on what we are trying to achieve — super intense and saturated colors with no dye bleed, chromatographic separation of dye mixtures, or muted and subtle shadings of color.'

Fiber Optic has a busy schedule of events. For Kimber interacting with customers in person fulfills her need to teach. 'It's the main thing I miss from my career as a research scientist. Being able to meet and talk with other fiber enthusiasts about our dyeing and products is, in its own way, the most direct form of teaching. I love talking about the chemistry, why we selected our fibers, and what we had in mind when we bring new products to market. It's very exciting for me when folks understand the chemistry behind the dyeing — when it stops being a simple black box. They never look at dyed yarn the same way.' It's also a chance to see what people make and

discuss their projects with them: 'I dream all the time about what people will make with our yarns — it's always a treat when folks take the time to bring finished items in to show me. If unsure about a substitution ask the dyer — most are thrilled to talk about their passion with someone interested.'

> ❝ I've never come home from a festival empty-handed or without a myriad of future ideas. ❞

The learning goes both ways: 'At a festival I get to talk to hundreds of people (customers, other vendors, instructors, designers) all of whom teach me of trends, colors, patterns, ideas, design elements, techniques … the list is endless. I try to be a sponge. I always come home with a treasure trove of business cards, notes, sketches, email addresses, buttons, spindles, knitting needles, pins, baskets, weavings, photos … a compilation of inspiration for future directions in my work. When I sit down and go through it later, all of these items serve as a breeding ground for creative ideas. I've never come home from a festival empty-handed or without a myriad of future ideas.'

Even for a company that attends so many festivals and events, Rhinebeck is special: 'I grew up in the Hudson Valley so, for me, vending at Rhinebeck is a little bit like coming home. Autumn is my favorite time of year and Rhinebeck in autumn is simply magical — cool, crisp autumn days, with trees at their peak of color. We try and get to the fairgrounds early to set up so that we can enjoy the transformation of the quiet empty fairgrounds into the bustling fiber festival. We are lucky because our booth location is close to where classes take place so it's common to have students stopping by to chat as we set up. Yes, it's a lot of effort, but to me, it's a lot like playing Santa on Christmas morning — a little bit of magic that's worth every moment of work when you see the faces of folks when they find that perfect item.'

'Talk with any and everyone who will talk to you – you'll be amazed at what you'll learn (and the friends you'll make – fiber folks are wonderful).'

— *Kimber Baldwin*

the Patterns

ABBREVIATIONS

beg	begin(ning)
bind off	aka cast off
BO	bind off aka cast off
CO	cast on
CC	contrast colour
dec	decrease
dpn(s)	double pointed needle(s)
EOR	end of round
est	established
inc	increase
k	knit
k2tog	knit 2 tog (a R leaning dec)
k3tog	knit 3 together (a R leaning double dec)
kfb	knit in the front and back of same st
m	stitch marker
m1	make one - pick up the strand between the needles with L needle tip from the front and knit into back of loop

m1L	make one left - pick up the strand between the needles with L needle tip from the front and knit into the back of loop
m1p	make one purl - pick up the strand between the needles with L needle tip from the front and purl into back of loop
m1R	make one right - pick up the strand between the needles with the L needle tip from the back and knit it normally
MC	main colour
p	purl
p2tog	purl 2 together
p2togtbl	purl 2 together through the back loop
patt	pattern
pm	place marker
rem	remain(ing)
rep	repeat(ing)

rnd(s)	round(s)
RS	right side
sl	slip X st(s) - sl sts purlwise individually with yarn at WS unless otherwise stated
slm	slip marker
ssk	slip, slip, knit - sl 2 sts knitwise individually, insert L needle into slipped sts at from from L to R, k these 2 sts tog (a L leaning dec)
sssk	slip, slip, slip, knit - sl 3 sts knitwise individually, insert L needle into slipped sts at from from L to R, k these 3 sts tog (a L leaning double dec)
st st	stockinette / stocking stitch
st(s)	stitch(es)
WS	wrong side
wyib	with yarn in back
wyif	with yarn in front
yo	yarn over

Jenny at the Fair

by Mary Jane Mucklestone

YARN

A non-superwash woolly wool yarn that blooms well. Starcroft Nash Island Light (175yds / 160m, 3.5 oz. / 100g) shown in MC: pine cone, CC1: lobster bake, CC2: acorn, CC3: finch and CC4: cove.

MC: 750[850, 900, 1000](1100, 1150, 1250)yds / 700[800, 850, 900](1000, 1050, 1150)m

CC1: 110[110, 110, 120] (120, 120, 120)yds / 100[100, 100, 110] (110, 110, 110)m

CC2: 75[75, 80, 80] (80, 85, 85)yds / 70[70, 75, 75] (75, 80, 80)m

CC3: 45[50, 50, 55] (60, 65, 70)yds / 45[50, 50, 55] (60, 65, 70)m

CC4: 45[45, 45, 50] (50, 50, 50)yds / 45[45, 45, 50] (50, 50, 50)m

NEEDLES AND NOTIONS

US 8 / 5mm 32" / 80cm or longer circular needle

US 8 / 5mm needles for you preferred method of working small circumferences in the rnd

US 9 / 5.5mm 32" / 80cm or longer circular needle

US 9 / 5.5mm for your preferred method of working small circumferences in the rnd

Stitch markers (one of a distinctive colour)

Five 1" / 25mm buttons

Scrap yarn

GAUGE

18 stitches and 22 rows = 4" / 10cm in colourwork and peerie patterns; use the needles necessary to match gauge for each.

SIZES

Finished chest circumference: 33[36½, 40, 43½] (47½, 51, 54½)" / 84[93, 103, 111] (121, 130, 139)cm.

Shown in size 36½" with 2" / 5cm of positive ease.

SCHEMATIC

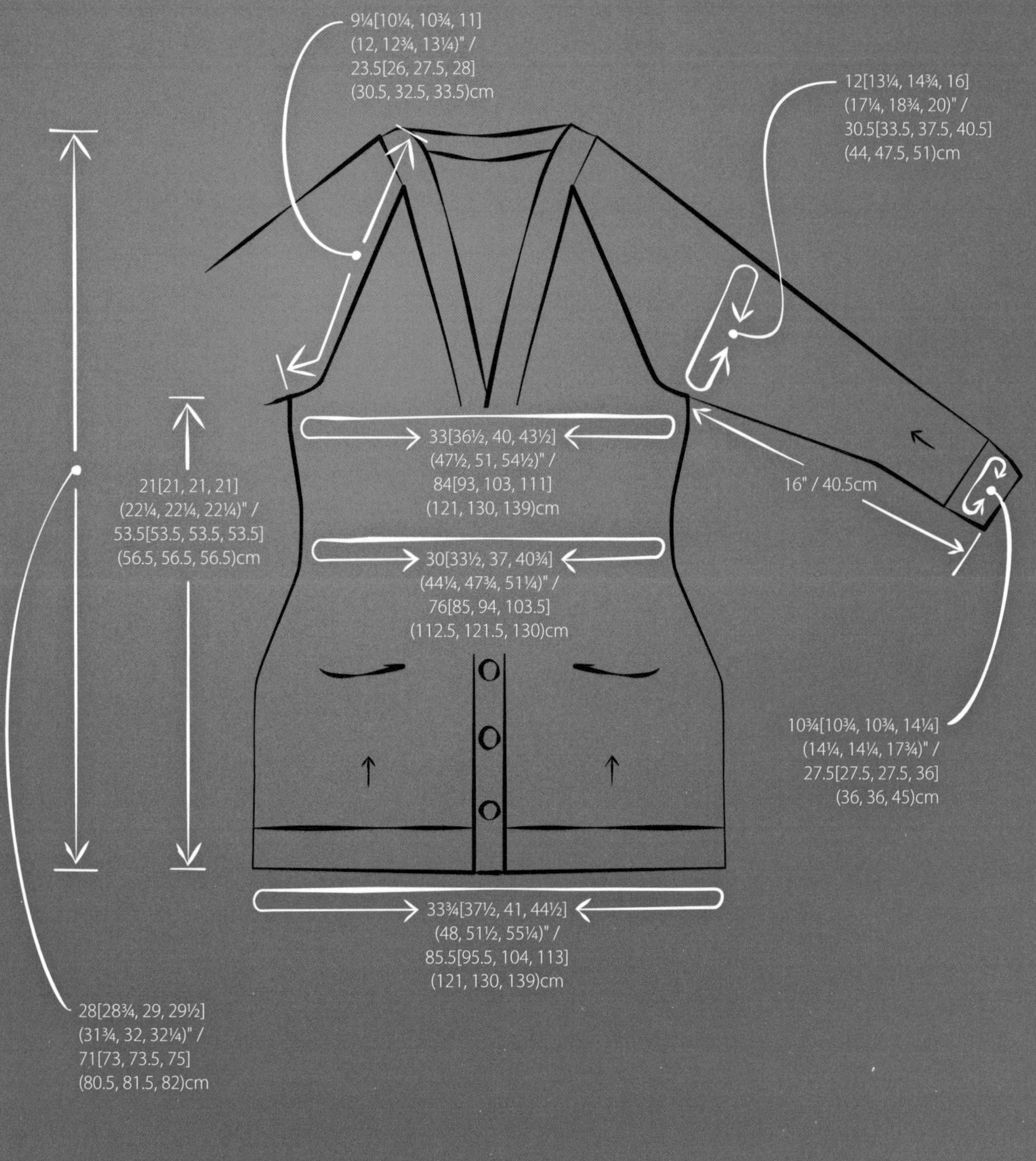

9¼[10¼, 10¾, 11]
(12, 12¾, 13¼)" /
23.5[26, 27.5, 28]
(30.5, 32.5, 33.5)cm

12[13¼, 14¾, 16]
(17¼, 18¾, 20)" /
30.5[33.5, 37.5, 40.5]
(44, 47.5, 51)cm

33[36½, 40, 43½]
(47½, 51, 54½)" /
84[93, 103, 111]
(121, 130, 139)cm

21[21, 21, 21]
(22¼, 22¼, 22¼)" /
53.5[53.5, 53.5, 53.5]
(56.5, 56.5, 56.5)cm

16" / 40.5cm

30[33½, 37, 40¾]
(44¼, 47¾, 51¼)" /
76[85, 94, 103.5]
(112.5, 121.5, 130)cm

10¾[10¾, 10¾, 14¼]
(14¼, 14¼, 17¾)" /
27.5[27.5, 27.5, 36]
(36, 36, 45)cm

33¾[37½, 41, 44½]
(48, 51½, 55¼)" /
85.5[95.5, 104, 113]
(121, 130, 139)cm

28[28¾, 29, 29½]
(31¾, 32, 32¼)" /
71[73, 73.5, 75]
(80.5, 81.5, 82)cm

Notes

STEEKING

A steek is a bridge of stitches that facilitates knitting a cardigan in the round. Knitting in the round means that the right side of the garment is always visible, making the colourwork pattern easy to follow, and there is no need to purl on the reverse side.

Each round will begin and end with three steek stitches (a total of six). All shaping directions occur within the rest of the garment, never in the steek. When the knitting is complete, two rows of simple crochet will be worked up the steek stitches and the work will be cut between them (it's not as scary as it sounds!) An additional benefit is that all of the loose ends from the frequent colour changes will be trapped within the steek.

Follow these guidelines for creating the steek:

- On all two-colour rounds, work the 6 steek sts alternating MC and CC.

- For rounds of a single colour, use that colour for all 6 steek sts.

- For Rnd 1 and Rnds 14-22 on border chart, use CC1 in place of MC in the steek.

Directions

BODY

Hem

With smaller needles, CO 152[168, 184, 200] (216, 232, 248) sts in MC. Work the following rows back and forth.

Row 1 (RS): k1, (k2, p2) to 3 sts from end, k3.

Row 2: p1, (p2, k2) to 3 sts from end, p3.

Repeat rows 1 and 2 for 2" / 5cm, ending with a WS row.

Bottom panel

Change to larger needles.

Set up Row (RS): using MC, k to end increasing 1 st mid-back, then create steek as follows: pm, CO 3 sts, pm to mark end of rnd, CO 3 sts, pm. Join to work in rnd, being careful not to twist stitches. 159[175, 191, 207] (223, 239, 255) sts.

Rnd 1: k3 steek sts, work border chart beginning with Rnd 1 to last 3 sts, k3 steek sts.

Work through Rnd 44 of border chart, working steek as directed in the notes.

Next rnd: with MC, k3, slm, k38[42, 46, 50] (54, 58, 62) (right front), pm, k77[85, 93, 101] (109, 117, 125) (back), pm, k38[42, 46, 50] (54, 58, 62) (left front), slm, k3. Set aside.

Pocket linings — make two

With smaller needles and CC4, provisionally cast on 18 sts. Work in st st until piece measures 5½" / 14cm. Place live stitches on hold.

Place pockets and begin waist shaping

Return to body and change to smaller needles if necessary to match gauge over peerie pattern.

Next rnd: with MC, k3, slm, k14[16, 19, 22] (24, 27, 30), place the next 18 sts on hold, and, with RS facing, slip held sts for pocket lining onto left needle and k across these 18 sts, *k to 3 sts before m, ssk, k1, slm, k1, k2tog, rep from * once more, k3[5, 6, 7] (9, 10, 11), place the next 18 sts on hold, k18 sts from second pocket lining in same way as first, k to end. 155[171, 187, 203] (219, 235, 251) sts.

K 3 rnds in MC.

Next rnd — dec rnd: k3, slm, *k to 3 sts before marker, ssk, k1, slm, k1, k2tog, repeat from * once more, k to m, slm, k3. 151[167, 183, 199] (215, 231, 247) sts.

Next rnd: Work in peerie pattern beginning with Row 1 and CC2 (see chart) to 6 sts before marker, k6 with MC, slm, k6 with MC, work peerie pattern across back to 6 sts before marker, k6 with MC, slm, k6 with MC, work peerie pattern to end. This row establishes the vertical alignment of the motifs; be sure to keep them aligned as you continue with the waist shaping. After completing the first set of peeries with CC2, follow with one peerie each of CC3, CC4, CC1, and CC2; use CC1 for the remainder of the garment.

Work even for 2 more rnds.

Next rnd: repeat dec rnd, working sts in colourwork patt as established.

Work 3 rnds even.

Rep last 4 rnds 2 more times, then repeat dec rnd once more. 135[151, 167, 183] (199, 215, 231) sts.

Work even for 16[16, 16, 16] (24, 24, 24) rnds.

Waist increases and beginning of neck shaping

**Next rnd: k3 steek sts, slm, k1, ssk, *k to 1 st before marker, m1R, k1, sl side m, k1, m1L, repeat from * once more, k to 3 sts before steek marker, k2tog, k1, slm, k3. 137[153, 169, 185] (201, 217, 233) sts.

Work even for 3 rounds.

Stitch Patterns

BORDER CHART

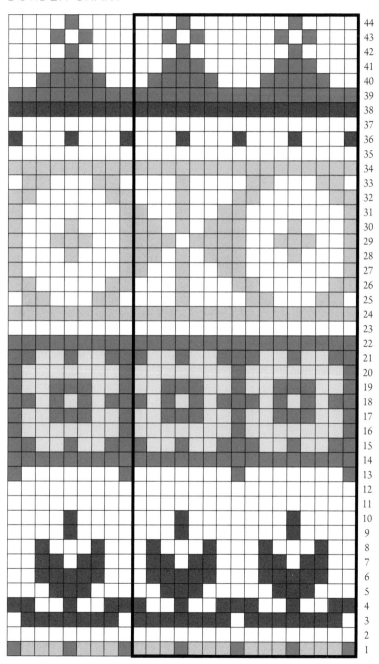

KEY

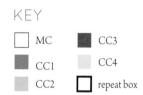

☐ MC	■ CC3
■ CC1	☐ CC4
▨ CC2	☐ repeat box

PEERIE CHART

On body: *rep sts within box to 1 st from end, work last st*

On sleeve: *rep st within box to end*

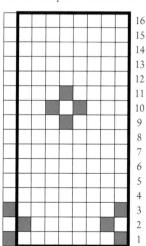

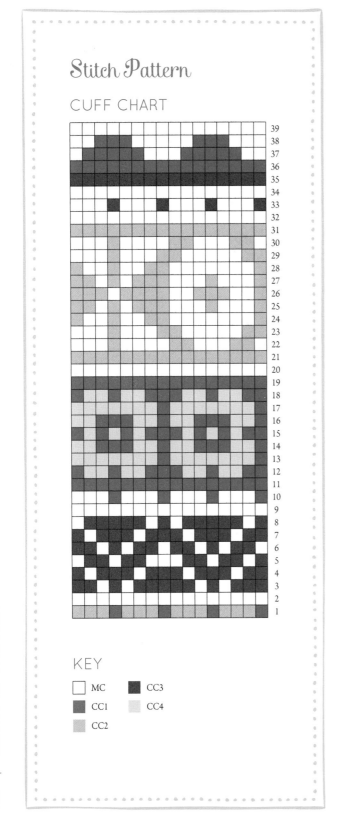

Stitch Pattern

CUFF CHART

(chart with rows numbered 1–39)

KEY

☐	MC	■	CC3
■	CC1	▨	CC4
▨	CC2		

Rep from ** 3 more times.

Next Rnd: k3, slm, k1, ssk, k to 3 sts before steek, k2tog, k1, slm, k3. 141[157, 173, 189] (205, 221, 237) sts. Set body aside.

SLEEVES — MAKE TWO

With smaller needles, CO 44[44, 44, 60] (60, 60, 76) sts in MC, join rnd, pm to mark end of rnd. Work (k2, p2) ribbing for 2" / 5cm.

Change to larger needles.

Set up rnd: using MC, k 1 rnd, increasing 4 sts evenly spaced. 48[48, 48, 64] (64, 64, 80) sts.

Work rnds 1-20 of cuff chart.

Begin sleeve shaping

Incorporate new sts into established colourwork pattern as you increase over the following rounds.

*Next rnd — inc rnd: k1, m1, k to 1 st before marker, m1, k1.

Work even for 15[7, 4, 11] (5, 3, 8) rnds.

Rep from * 1[4, 7, 2] (5,8, 3) more times; work inc rnd once more. 54[60, 66, 72] (78, 84, 90) sts.

Change to smaller needles, if necessary to maintain gauge, and work remainder of sleeve rnds from peerie chart using CC1 for peeries.

Work even until sleeve measures approximately 16" / 40.5 cm or desired length and pattern corresponds with last row on body. K5[6, 7, 7] (8, 9, 10) sts beyond marker and cut yarn, leaving a long tail. Place 44[48, 52, 58] (62, 66, 70) sleeve sts on hold, and the remaining 10[12, 14, 14] (16, 18, 20) underarm sts on a piece of scrap yarn.

YOKE

Join body and sleeves

Continue peerie pattern as established in the fronts, back, and sleeves in all of the following yoke rounds, eliminating any peerie sts that fall within 3 sts of the shaping markers.

All sizes except 51 and 54"

With the needles needed to obtain gauge in the peerie pattern, using MC, k3 steek sts, slm, k26[29, 32, 36] (39, -, -), *place next 10[12, 14, 14] (16, -, -) sts on scrap yarn, pm, k44[48, 52, 58] (62, -, -) sleeve sts, pm*, k63[69, 75, 83] (89, -, -) sts across back, rep from * to * for second sleeve, k26[29, 32, 36] (39, -, -), slm, k3 steek sts. 209[229, 249, 277] (297, -, -) sts.

Work 2 rnds even.

Sizes 51 and 54" only

With the needles needed to obtain gauge in the peerie pattern, using MC, k3 steek sts, slm, k-[-, -, -] (-, 39, 42), k2tog, k1, *place next -[-, -, -] (-, 18, 20) sts on scrap yarn, pm, then from sleeve k1, ssk, k-[-, -, -] (-, 60, 64), k2tog, k1, pm*, then across back k1, ssk, k-[-, -, -, -] (-, 89, 95), k2tog, k1, rep from * to * for second sleeve, k1, ssk, k-[-, -, -] (-, 39, 42), slm, k3 steek sts.-[-, -, -] (-, 309, 329) sts.

Next rnd: k3, slm, *k to 3 sts before marker, k2tog, k1, slm, k1, ssk, rep from * three more times, k to marker, slm, k3. -[-, -, -] (-, 301, 321) sts.

Work 1 rnd even.

All sizes

Next rnd — Dec Rnd A: k3 steek sts, slm, k1, ssk, *k to 3 sts before marker, k2tog, k1, slm, k1, ssk, rep from * three more times, k to 3 sts before marker, k2tog, k1, slm, k3 steek sts. 199[219, 239, 267] (287, 291, 311) sts.

Work 1 rnd even.

Next rnd — Dec Rnd B: k3 steek sts, slm, *k to 3 sts before marker, k2tog, k1, slm, k1, ssk, rep from * three more times, k to marker, slm, k3 steek sts. 191[211, 231, 259] (279, 283, 303) sts.

Work even for 1 round.

Continue decreasing at raglan markers every other round (Dec Round B), and decreasing at neck edge (Dec Round A) every 6th[6th, 4th, 4th] (4th, 4th, 4th) round until 2[2, 0, 3] (2, 2, 4) sts remain on fronts. 53[55, 59 79] (79, 75, 87) sts and 39[43, 45, 47] (51, 53, 55) rnds. BO loosely, maintaining decreases at raglans and neck edge within the bind off. Include steek in bind off.

CUTTING THE STEEK

Prepare the steek for cutting by working two lines of slip-stitch crochet as follows:

There are 6 stitches in the steek. You will join the 2nd and 3rd stitches together with one line of crochet and the 4th and 5th stitches together with the second. Then you will be able to cut safely between the 3rd and 4th stitch.

Turn your sweater so that the right front is nearest to you, with RS facing. Make a slip knot with any CC and place it on the crochet hook. *Insert the hook through one leg of the second stitch and one leg of the third stitch. Wrap the yarn around the hook, pull it through the stitch and through the loop on the hook, rep from * in each row until you reach the top of the steek, then cut the yarn and secure the end. Turn the work 180 degrees, so the left front of the garment is nearest you and repeat from * to *.

With sharp scissors, carefully cut down the centre of the steek, between the centre two stitches. The cut edges will naturally roll to the wrong side along the crocheted stitches making a neat finish.

BUTTONBAND

With smaller needle (the longest circular needle available) and MC, between the outermost steek stitch and the first body stitch, pick up and knit 3 sts for every 4 rows along right front edge, then 1 st for each bound off st at the shoulders and back neck, and again 3 sts for every 4 rows along the left front edge. Adjust the total number of sts to a multiple of 4.

Row 1 (WS): sl1, (p2, k2) until 3 sts from end, p3.

Row 2: sl1, (k2, p2) until 3 sts from end, k3.

Rep rows 1-2 once more. Keeping in established rib patt, work 5 three-stitch buttonholes evenly spaced along right front edge; beg first buttonhole in 4th st from lower edge and last buttonhole at first neck shaping decrease.

One row button holes

Sl1 wyif, bring yarn to back, *sl1, psso, rep from * twice, sl st on right needle to left and turn work. Cable cast on 3 sts, bring yarn to front between needles and cast on 1 more st; turn work. Sl1 kwise and pass last cast on st over it.

Work (k2, p2) ribbing for 8 rows from beginning. Bind off in patt.

FINISHING

Pocket edging

Transfer the held sts for the first pocket onto smaller needle. Work the following rows flat, with MC.

Row 1 (RS): p.

Row 2: k.

BO in purl stitch.

Sew pocket sides to WS of sweater, carefully undo the provisional cast-on at bottom edge and sew live stitches into place.

Repeat for second pocket.

Weave in all ends and block to measurements. Sew on buttons opposite the buttonholes.

Dutchess

by Cheryl Burke

YARN

A worsted weight yarn with crisp stitch definition that will show off the strong yoke design is ideal, wool or wool blends with a bit of elasticity will work best. While the pullover is shown in a superwash wool, any smooth yarn, such as a worsted spun untreated wool should work for the crisply geometric colourwork. I recommend swatching the yoke pattern to see how your colours will work together, the results can often be surprising.

Shown in Shelridge Farm W4 (100% wool, 220yds/201m, 3.5oz/100g) in MC: Bordeaux and CC: Spanish Moss.

MC: 1025[1100, 1210, 1255, 1350] (1470, 1545, 1595, 1675) [1775, 1875, 1950, 2015]yds / 935[1000, 1100, 1145, 1230] (1340, 1405, 1450, 1525) [1615, 1705, 1775, 1835]m.

CC: 90[95, 100, 110, 120] (120, 125, 140, 165) [165, 195, 205, 220]yds / 80[85, 90, 100, 110] (110, 114, 130, 150) [150, 175, 185, 200]m.

NEEDLES AND NOTIONS

US 7 / 4.5mm 24" / 60cm or longer circular needle

US 7 / 4.5mm dpns or circulars for your preferred method of working small circumferences in the rnd

Stitch markers

Scrap yarn for holding stitches

GAUGE

20 sts and 28 rnds = 4" / 10cm in st st in the rnd.

20 sts and 24 rnds = 4" / 10cm in colourwork.

SIZES

Finished chest circumference: 32[34, 37, 39, 42] (44, 47, 49, 52) [54, 57, 59, 62]" / 81.5[86.5, 94, 99, 106.5] (112, 119.5, 124.5, 132) [137, 145, 150, 157.5]cm.

Shown in size 39" with 2" / 5cm of positive ease.

SCHEMATIC

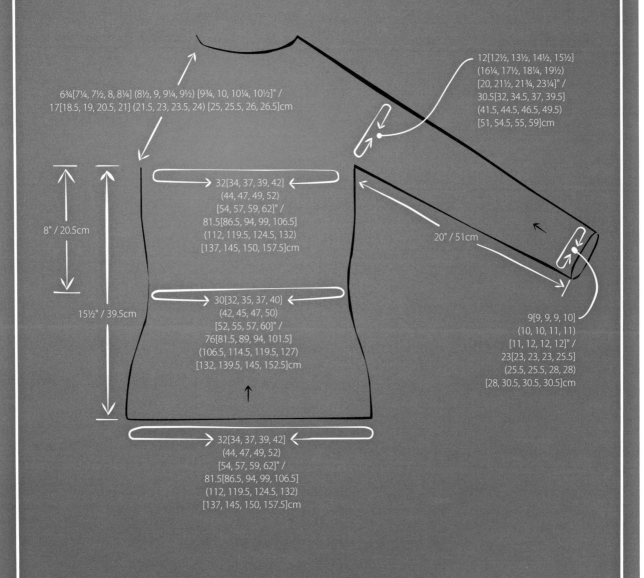

6¾[7¼, 7½, 8, 8¼] (8½, 9, 9¼, 9½) [9¾, 10, 10¼, 10½]" /
17[18.5, 19, 20.5, 21] (21.5, 23, 23.5, 24) [25, 25.5, 26, 26.5]cm

12[12½, 13½, 14½, 15½]
(16¼, 17½, 18¼, 19½)
[20, 21½, 21¾, 23¼]" /
30.5[32, 34.5, 37, 39.5]
(41.5, 44.5, 46.5, 49.5)
[51, 54.5, 55, 59]cm

8" / 20.5cm

32[34, 37, 39, 42]
(44, 47, 49, 52)
[54, 57, 59, 62]" /
81.5[86.5, 94, 99, 106.5]
(112, 119.5, 124.5, 132)
[137, 145, 150, 157.5]cm

20" / 51cm

15½" / 39.5cm

30[32, 35, 37, 40]
(42, 45, 47, 50)
[52, 55, 57, 60]" /
76[81.5, 89, 94, 101.5]
(106.5, 114.5, 119.5, 127)
[132, 139.5, 145, 152.5]cm

9[9, 9, 9, 10]
(10, 10, 11, 11)
[11, 12, 12, 12]" /
23[23, 23, 23, 25.5]
(25.5, 25.5, 28, 28)
[28, 30.5, 30.5, 30.5]cm

32[34, 37, 39, 42]
(44, 47, 49, 52)
[54, 57, 59, 62]" /
81.5[86.5, 94, 99, 106.5]
(112, 119.5, 124.5, 132)
[137, 145, 150, 157.5]cm

Stitch Patterns

CARTRIDGE RIBBING
worked over a multiple of 5 sts in the rnd

Row 1: (k2, p3) rep to end.

Row 2: k3, (p1, k4) rep to 2 sts from end, p1, k1.

YOKE CHART

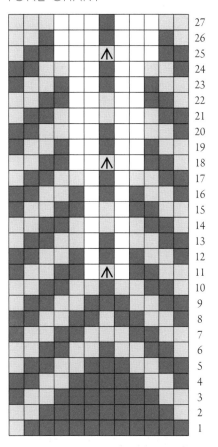

27
26
25
24
23
22
21
20
19
18
17
16
15
14
13
12
11
10
9
8
7
6
5
4
3
2
1

KEY

⋀ slip 2 sts tog knitwise, k1, lift slipped sts over just worked (a centered double dec)

▨ MC

▨ CC

☐ no stitch

Directions

BODY

With MC and circular needle CO 160[170, 185, 195, 210] (220, 235, 245, 260) [270, 285, 295, 310] sts. Join rnd and pm for end of rnd.

Work in cartridge ribbing for 2.5" / 6.5cm ending with rnd 2.

Sizes 32, 34, 42, 44, 52, 54, and 62" only

Next rnd: k80[85, -, -, 105] (110, -, -, 130) [135, -, -, 155], pm, k to end.

Sizes 37, 39, 47, 49, 57 and 59" only

Next rnd: k-[-, 91, 96, -] (-, 116, 121, -) [-, 141, 146, -], k2tog, pm, k to end. 160[170, 184, 194, 210] (220, 234, 244, 260) [270, 284, 294, 310] sts.

All sizes

K 4 rnds.

Waist decreases

Next rnd — dec rnd: k1, ssk, k to 3 sts from m, k2tog, k1, slm, k1, ssk, k to 3 sts from end, k2tog, k1.

K 14 rnds.

Repeat last 15 rnds once more.

Work dec rnd once more. 148[158, 172, 182, 198] (208, 222, 232, 248) [258, 272, 282, 298] sts rem.

K 5 rnds.

Bust increases

Next rnd — dec rnd: k1, m1L, k to 1 st from m, m1R, k1, slm, k1, m1L, k to 1 st from end, m1R.

K 14 rnds.

Repeat last 15 rnds once more.

Work inc rnd once more. 160[170, 184, 194, 210] (220, 234, 244, 260) [270, 284, 294, 310] sts.

Work in st st until body measures 15.5" / 39.5 cm from CO edge; on last round stop 7[7, 7, 8, 9] (9, 10, 10, 11) [11, 12, 12, 13] sts from EOR. Put body aside while working on sleeves; do not cut yarn.

SLEEVES

With MC and dpns (or preferred needles for working small circumferences in the rnd) CO 45[45, 45, 45, 50] (50, 50, 55, 55) [55, 60, 60, 60] sts. Join rnd and pm to mark end of rnd. Work in Cartridge Ribbing for 2.5" / 6.5cm ending with rnd 2.

K 1 rnd.

*Next rnd — inc rnd: k1, m1L, work until 1 st before EOR, m1R, k1.

K 15[13, 9, 8, 7] (7, 5, 5, 4) [4, 4, 4, 3] rnds.

Rep from * 7[8, 11, 12, 13] (14, 18, 17, 20) [22, 22, 23, 27] more times. 61[63, 69, 71, 78] (80, 88, 91, 97) [101, 106, 108, 116] sts.

Work in st st until sleeve measures 20" / 51 cm from CO, or desired length to underarm, on last round stop 7[7, 7, 8, 9] (9, 10, 10, 11) [11, 12, 12, 13] sts from EOR. Slip next 13[13, 14, 15, 17] (17, 19, 20, 21) [22, 23, 23, 25] sts to scrap yarn for underarm, put remaining 48[50, 55, 56, 61] (63, 69, 71, 76) [79, 83, 85, 91] sts on hold.

YOKE

Return to held stitches for body.

Next rnd: *slip 13[13, 14, 15, 17] (17, 19, 20, 21) [22, 23, 23, 25] body sts onto scrap yarn for the underarm, removing marker, and, using yarn from body, k across k24[25, 27, 28, 30] (31, 34, 35, 38) [39, 41, 42, 45] sts of sleeve, pm, k rem sleeve sts* k across 67[72,78, 82, 88] (93, 98, 102, 109) [113, 119, 124, 130] body sts to 7[7, 7, 8, 9] (9, 10, 10, 11) [11, 12, 12, 13] before next marker, rep from * to * k to end. K to marker on sleeve; this marks the new EOR, the opposite marker is referred to as the side marker. 115[122, 133, 138, 149] (156, 167, 173, 185) [192, 202, 209, 221] sts between each pair of markers.

The following row adjusts the total number of stitches to a multiple of 12 to prepare for the colourwork. Increase or decrease as follows for your size. Afterwards you will have 114[120, 132, 138, 150] (156, 168, 174, 186) [192, 204, 210, 222] sts between each pair of markers and 228[240, 264, 276, 300] (312, 336, 348, 372) [384, 408, 420, 444] sts total.

Sizes 32, 34 and 37" only

Next rnd: dec 1[2, 1, -, -] (-, -, -, -) [-, -, -, -] sts on both the front and on the back.

Sizes 42, 47, 49, 52, 57, 59 and 62" only

Next rnd: inc -[-, -, -, 1] (-, 1, 1, 1) [-, 2, 1, 1] sts on both the front and on the back.

Sizes 39, 44 and 54" only

K 1 rnd.

All sizes

Work short rows back and forth to raise the back of neck. When directed to "turn," remember to prepare the work so that the gap can later be closed. Cheryl used the wrap and turn method, but other methods, such as the wrapless turn, can be worked if preferred.

Row 1 (RS): k10 sts, turn.

Row 2 (WS): p around the back to 10 sts past the side marker, turn.

Row 3: k to 12 sts from gap, turn.

Row 4: p to 12 sts from gap, turn.

Repeat rows 3 and 4 once more. 3 turning points on each side.

K 1 rnd, closing gaps as you come to them, and removing side marker.

WRAPLESS SHORT ROWS

Preparing the gap: at turning point turn work and place a piece of scrap yarn over the working yarn; work the next stitch making sure the scrap yarn is caught between the two rows.

Closing the gap — RS rows: work to the turning point, including the stitch directly above the scrap yarn; pull on both ends of the scrap yarn and place resulting loop onto left needle; knit loop together with following stitch.

Closing the gap — WS rows: work to the turning point, including the stitch directly above the scrap yarn; slip the next stitch purlwise; pull on both ends of the scrap yarn and place resulting loop onto left needle; return slipped stitch to left needle and purl it together with loop.

Next rnd - reposition start of round to centre colourwork design: remove EOR marker, k3[0, 5, 3, 2] (5, 5, 2, 3) [5, 5, 2, 2] sts, replace EOR marker.

K 3[6, 9, 9, 9] (9, 12, 12, 12) [12, 12, 12, 12] rnds.

Knit 27 rnds from yoke chart. 114[120, 132, 138, 150] (156, 168, 174, 186) [192, 204, 210, 222] sts.

Break MC and continue with CC.

Next rnd: *k26[10, 4, 4, 6] (6, 5, 5, 4) [4, 4, 3, 3], k2tog, rep from * 3[9, 21, 22, 17] (17, 23, 23, 30) [31, 33, 41, 43] more times, k rem 2[0, 0, 0, 6] (12, 0, 6, 0) [0, 0, 0, 2] sts. 110[110, 110, 115, 132] (138, 144, 150, 155) [160, 170, 168, 178] sts.

K 5[5, 4, 7, 3] (3, 6, 4, 7) [3, 4, 5, 6] rnds.

Sizes 42" and larger only

Next rnd: *k-[-, -, -, 5] (5, 4, 4, 4) [6, 5, 6, 6], k2tog, rep from * -[-, -, -, 16] (17, 23, 23, 24) [17, 22, 19, 21] more times, k rem -[-, -, -, 13] (12, 0, 5, 5) [16, 9, 8, 2] sts. -[-, -, -, 115] (120, 120, 126, 130) [142, 147, 148, 156] sts.

K -[-, -, -, 4] (3, 5, 4, 5) [3, 4, 5, 6] rnds.

Sizes 54" and larger only

Next rnd: *k-[-, -, -, -] (-, -, -, -) [10, 10, 9, 8], k2tog, rep from * -[-, -, -, -] (-, -, -, -) [10, 11, 12, 14] more times, k -[-, -, -, -] (-, -, -, -) [8, 3, 5, 4] sts, -[-, -, -, -] (-, -, -, -) [k2tog, -, -, k2tog].

-[-, -, -, -] (-, -, -, -) [130, 135, 135, 140] sts.

K -[-, -, -, -] (-, -, -, -) [4, 6, 6, 5] rnds.

NECKBAND

Work in cartridge ribbing until neckline measures ¾" / 2cm for sizes 32–42" and 1" / 2.5cm for sizes 44–62". Bind off.

FINISHING

Weave underarm sts together with the Kitchener stitch. Weave in ends. Block to finished measurements.

YARN

Sugarleaf is worked in a woolen-spun wool yarn that blooms beautifully when washed, giving the colourwork yoke a smooth, unified look and the body of the sweater a cozy feel.

Shown in Green Mountain Spinnery New Mexico Organic (100% wool, 180yds / 165m, 2.0oz/57g) and Local Color (100% wool, 180yds / 165m, 2.0oz/ 57g). Local Color is the plant dyed version of the undyed New Mexico Organic.

MC — New Mexico Organic, Grey; CC — Local Color, Tomato

MC: 1000[1045, 1110, 1225, 1245] (1325, 1375, 1400, 1530) [1595, 1660, 1720]yds / 915[955, 1015, 1120, 1140] (1215, 1260, 1320, 1400) [1460, 1520, 1575]m

CC: 100[100, 110, 110, 110] (130, 130, 130, 150) [150, 150, 170] yds / 95[95, 100, 100, 100] (120, 120, 120, 140) [140, 140, 155]m

NEEDLES AND NOTIONS

US 4 / 3.5mm 32" / 80cm or longer circular needle

US 4 / 3.5mm dpns or circulars for your preferred method of working small circumferences in the rnd

Nine locking or split ring stitch markers

Scrap yarn

Nine 1¼" / 3cm toggle buttons; shown with Melissa Jean large rosewood toggles.

GAUGE

21 sts and 32 rows = 4" / 10cm st st

21 sts and 28 rows = 4" / 10cm over colourwork pattern

Check gauge over both patterns and if necessary use a larger needle size for the colourwork rows.

SIZES

Finished chest circumference: 32[34, 36, 38, 40] (42, 44, 46, 48) [50, 52, 54]" / 81[86, 91, 97, 102] (107, 112, 117, 122, 127) [137, 142, 147]cm.

Shown in size 40" with zero ease.

Sugarleaf

by Mary-Heather Cogar

SCHEMATIC

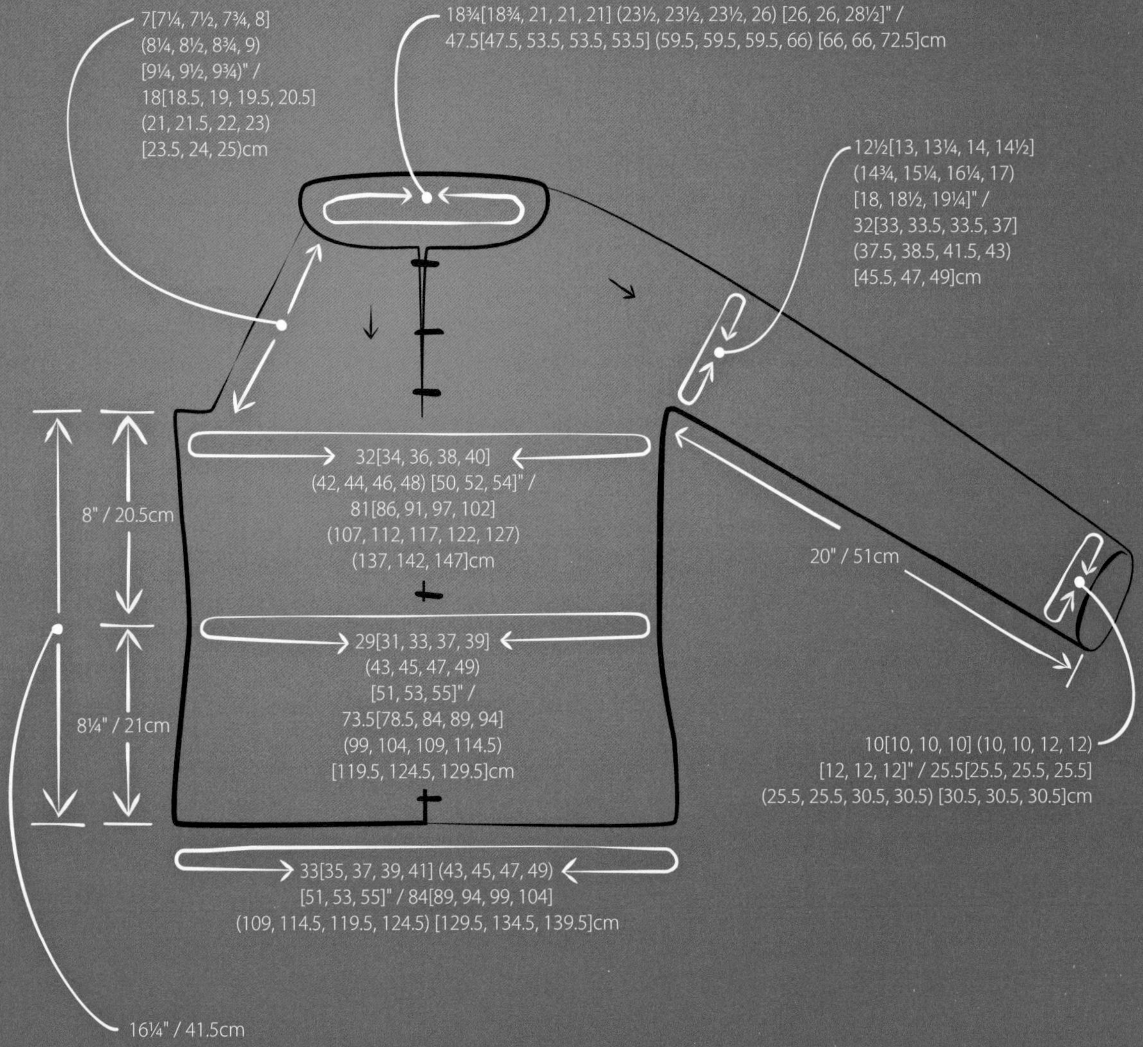

7[7¼, 7½, 7¾, 8]
(8¼, 8½, 8¾, 9)
[9¼, 9½, 9¾]" /
18[18.5, 19, 19.5, 20.5]
(21, 21.5, 22, 23)
[23.5, 24, 25]cm

18¾[18¾, 21, 21, 21] (23½, 23½, 23½, 26) [26, 26, 28½]" /
47.5[47.5, 53.5, 53.5, 53.5] (59.5, 59.5, 59.5, 66) [66, 66, 72.5]cm

12½[13, 13¼, 14, 14½]
(14¾, 15¼, 16¼, 17)
[18, 18½, 19¼]" /
32[33, 33.5, 33.5, 37]
(37.5, 38.5, 41.5, 43)
[45.5, 47, 49]cm

8" / 20.5cm

32[34, 36, 38, 40]
(42, 44, 46, 48) [50, 52, 54]" /
81[86, 91, 97, 102]
(107, 112, 117, 122, 127)
(137, 142, 147]cm

20" / 51cm

8¼" / 21cm

29[31, 33, 37, 39]
(43, 45, 47, 49)
[51, 53, 55]" /
73.5[78.5, 84, 89, 94]
(99, 104, 109, 114.5)
[119.5, 124.5, 129.5]cm

10[10, 10, 10] (10, 10, 12, 12)
[12, 12, 12]" / 25.5[25.5, 25.5, 25.5]
(25.5, 25.5, 30.5, 30.5) [30.5, 30.5, 30.5]cm

33[35, 37, 39, 41] (43, 45, 47, 49)
[51, 53, 55]" / 84[89, 94, 99, 104]
(109, 114.5, 119.5, 124.5) [129.5, 134.5, 139.5]cm

16¼" / 41.5cm

Stitch Pattern

YOKE

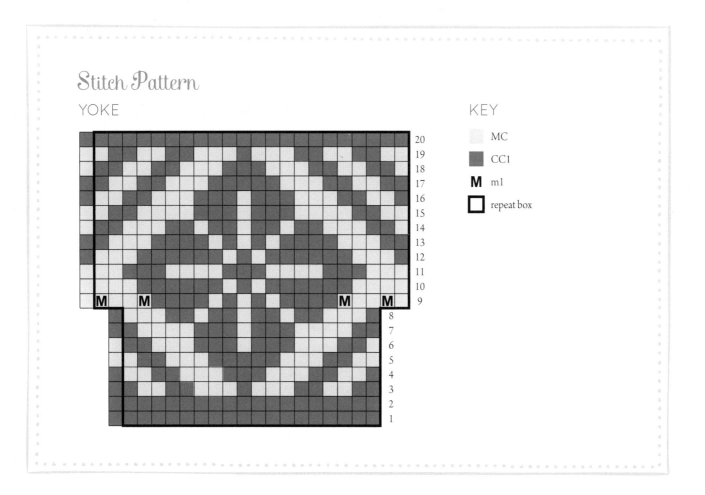

KEY

░	MC
■	CC1
M	m1
☐	repeat box

Notes

Sugarleaf's body is worked back and forth in one piece, from the top circular yoke colourwork section down. Sleeves are picked up after the body is worked and knit seamlessly from underarms to the cuff. The cuffs and hem are trimmed with a garter rib, and a simple I-cord bind-off along the fronts and neck of the cardigan makes a tidy edging. Toggle buttons made from rich, smooth rosewood strike a lovely balance between rustic and sophisticated.

Sugarleaf is designed to be worn with 0–2" (0–5cm) positive ease. Negative ease is not recommended, as it will likely cause gaping at the buttonholes. Waist shaping and optional short-rows in the bust give this cozy, classic cardigan a flattering fit.

The pattern includes short row bust darts for a more flattering fit on curvier figures. If your underbust and full bust measurements differ by less than four inches (10cm), simply omit the dart.

Directions

YOKE

Using MC, CO 98[98, 98, 112, 112] (112, 126, 126, 126) [140, 140, 140] sts. Beginning with a purl row, work 3 rows st st.

Next row: k7[7, 7, 8, 8] (8, 9, 9, 9)[10, 10, 10], (m1, k3) to last 7[7, 7, 8, 8] (8, 9, 9, 9)[10, 10, 10] sts, m1, k to end. 127[127, 127, 145, 145] (145, 163, 163, 163) [181, 181, 181] sts.

Purl 1 row.

Join CC and work rows 1-20 from yoke chart. 155[155, 155, 177, 177] (177, 199, 199, 199) [221, 221, 221] sts.

Next row (CC): k2[2, 2, 3, 3] (3, 2, 2, 2) [3, 3, 3], (m1, k4) to last 1[1, 1, 2, 2] (2, 1, 1, 1) [2, 2, 2] sts, m1, k to end. 194[194, 194, 221, 221] (221, 249, 249, 249) [276, 276, 276] sts.

Break off CC. Using MC, and beginning with a WS row, work 5[5, 7, 9, 7] (9, 9, 9, 9) [11, 11, 11] rows st st.

Next Row: k2[2, 2, 3, 3] (3, 2, 2, 2) [3, 3, 3], (m1, k5) to 2[2, 2, 3, 3] (3, 2, 2, 2) [3, 3, 3] sts from end, m1, k to end. 233[233, 233, 265, 265] (265, 299, 299, 299) [331, 331, 331] sts.

Work 5[7, 7, 7, 9] (9, 11, 11, 13) [13, 13, 13] rows st st.

Next row: k, increasing 9[25, 31, 7, 15] (21, 1, 13, 19) [3, 5, 5] sts evenly across row. 242[258, 264, 272, 280] (286, 300, 312, 318) [334, 336, 336] sts.

Place markers for short-row and raglan shaping

Next row (WS): p34[37, 38, 40, 41] (43, 45, 47, 47) [50, 50, 51], pm, p53[56, 56, 57, 58] (58, 60, 63, 65) [68, 68, 67], pm, p68[72, 76, 78, 82] (84, 90, 92, 94) [98, 100, 100], pm, p53[56, 56, 57, 58] (58, 60, 63, 65) [68, 68, 67], pm, p rem 34[37, 38, 40, 41] (43, 45, 47, 47) [50, 50, 51] sts.

Short row shaping to lower front neckline

When directed to 'turn', remember to prepare the work so that the gap can later be closed. Mary-Heather used the wrap and turn method, but other methods, such as the wrapless turn (see page 123), can be worked if preferred.

Note: 'final marker' refers to the last marker you come to on the current row.

Next row (RS): k to final marker, slm, k4, turn.

Next row: p to final marker, slm, p4, turn.

Next row: k to 5 sts before previous gap, turn.

Next row: p to 5 sts before previous gap, turn.

Repeat last 2 rows 3 more times. 5 turning points on each side.

Next row: k to end, closing gaps as you come to them.

Next row: p to end, closing gaps as you come to them.

Work 2 rows in st st.

Raglan increases

Next row (RS): *k to 1 st before marker, m1L, k1, slm, k1, m1R, rep from * 3 more times, k to end.

Next row: purl.

Rep last 2 rows 1[1, 1, 1, 2] (2, 2, 2, 3) [3, 4, 5] more times. 258[274, 280, 288, 304] (310, 324, 336, 350) [366, 376, 384] sts.

BODY

Divide for fronts, back, and sleeves:

Next row (RS): *k to marker, remove marker, cable CO 4[4, 5, 6, 6] (7, 7, 8, 9) [9, 10, 11], pm, CO 4[4, 5, 6, 6] (7, 7, 8, 9) [9, 10, 11], slip 57[60, 60, 61, 64] (64, 66, 69, 73) [76, 78, 79] sleeve sts onto scrap yarn, remove marker, rep from * once more, k to end.

40[43, 45, 48, 50] (53, 55, 58, 60) [63, 65, 68] front sts (each side), 80[84, 90, 94, 100] (104, 110, 114, 120) [124, 130, 134] back sts. 160[170, 180, 190, 200] (210, 220, 230, 240) [250, 260, 270] total sts.

Work 11 rows in st st.

Bust short rows — optional

If not working bust darts work 2 more rows even and proceed to Waist Shaping.

Next row (RS): k to 20 sts before side marker, turn.

Next row: p to end.

Next row: k to gap, close gap, k4, turn.

Next row: p to end.

Rep last 2 rows 2 more times. 4 turning points.

Next row: k to end, closing gap when you come to it.

Next row: p to 20 sts before side marker, turn.

Next row: k to end.

Next row: p to gap, close gap, p4, turn.

Next row: k to end.

Rep last 2 rows 2 more times. 4 turning points.

Next row: p to end, closing gap when you come to it.

Waist shaping

Next row (RS): *k to 4 sts before marker, k2tog, k2, slm, k2, ssk, rep from * once more, k to end.

Work 11 rows in st st.

Rep last 12 rows 3 more times. 144[154, 164, 174, 184] (194, 204, 214, 224) [234, 244, 254] sts.

Next row (RS): *k to 2 sts before marker, m1L, k2, slm, k2, m1R, rep from * once more, k to end.

Work 11 rows in st st.

Rep last 12 rows 4 more times. 164[174, 184, 194, 204] (214, 224, 234, 244) [254, 264, 274] total sts.

Next row: k to end.

Garter rib

Row 1 (WS): p3, (k3, p2) to last st, p1

Row 2: knit

Rep last 2 rows 7 more times.

Bind off loosely.

SLEEVES

Remove scrap yarn and slip held sts for sleeve onto dpns (or preferred needles for working small circumferences in the rnd).

Join yarn and pick up and k 10[10, 12, 14, 14] (16, 16, 18, 20) [20, 22, 24] sts — this should be 1 st for every cast on st and an extra st at each end, which should help to reduce any holes. K around to the centre of the picked up sts, pm to mark end of rnd.

Next rnd: k4[4, 5, 6, 6] (7, 7, 8, 9) [9, 10, 11], ssk, k to 6[6, 7, 8, 8] (9, 9, 10, 11) [11, 12, 13] sts from end, k2tog, k to end. 65[68, 70, 73, 76] (78, 80, 85, 91) [94, 98, 101] sts.

*Knit 17[13, 11, 13, 10] (9, 10, 8, 8) [7, 6, 6] rnds.

Next rnd: k1, k2tog, k to 3 sts from end, ssk, k1.

Repeat from * 6[7, 8, 8, 9] (10, 9, 12, 12) [14, 15, 16] more times. 51[52, 52, 55, 56] (56, 60, 59, 63) [64, 64, 67] sts.

Sizes 34, 36, 40, 42, 44, 50 and 52" only

Knit -[13, 11, -, 10] (9, 10, -, -) [7, 6, -] rnds.

Next rnd – dec rnd: k1, k2tog, k to end. 51[51, 51, 55, 55] (55, 59, 59, 63) [63, 63, 67] sts.

All sizes

Work even until sleeve measures 17" / 43cm or 4" / 10cm shorter than total desired length.

Work rnds 1 to 21 of sleeve chart for appropriate sleeve.

Break CC. 49[49, 49, 53, 53] (53, 57, 57, 61) [61, 61, 65] sts.

Next rnd: using MC, k, decreasing 4 [4, 4, 3, 3] (3, 2, 2, 1) [1, 1, 0] sts evenly spaced around. 45 [45, 45, 50, 50] (50, 55, 55, 60) [60, 60, 65] sts.

Stitch Patterns

LEFT CUFF

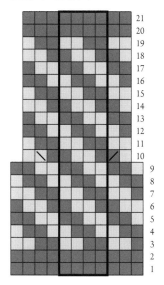

RIGHT CUFF

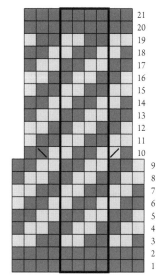

KEY

▨ MC	╱ k2tog	☐ repeat box
▧ CC1	╲ ssk	

Garter rib cuff

Rnd 1: (p3, k2) around.

Rnd 2: knit.

Rep last 2 rnds 3 more times.

Bind off loosely.

I-CORD EDGING

Using split ring stitch markers or scrap yarn, mark the desired placement of 9 buttons down the right front edge. These markers will indicate where you will work I-cord loops for buttonholes while working the I-cord bind-off.

With RS facing, pick up and knit 2 sts for every 3 rows up right front, pick up and knit 1 st for every st around neck, pick up and knit 2 sts for every 3 rows down left front.

Next row (WS): p to end.

Work I-cord with button loops as follows:

Next row: CO 3 sts, and begin I-cord bind-off: *k2, k2tog through the back loop, slip 3 sts from RH needle back to LH needle, rep from * to marker; remove marker and **k3, slip 3 sts from RH needle back to LH needle, rep from ** 4 more times to complete I-cord button loop, rep from * until all 9 button loops have been worked; continue working I-cord bind-off to the last 3 sts. Slip these 3 sts back to LH needle, sl1, k2tog, psso. Break yarn and draw through remaining st.

FINISHING

Sew buttons to I-cord on left front to match buttonholes. Weave in ends. Soak and block to measurements shown.

· · · · · · • · · · · · ·

YARN

Worsted weight yarn with good stitch definition in wool or wool blends are recommended. Shown in Green Mountain Spinnery Weekend Wool (100% wool, 140yds / 128m, 2.3oz / 64g) in Lichen.

1075[1170, 1250, 1330, 1410, 1500] (1570, 1650, 1740, 1810, 1900)yds / 985[1070, 1145, 1215, 1290, 1370] (1435, 1510, 1590, 1655, 1735)m.

NEEDLES AND NOTIONS

US 7 / 4.5mm 32" / 80cm circular needle

US 8 / 5mm 32" / 80cm circular needle or longer

US 8 / 5mm dpns or circulars for your preferred method of knitting small circumferences in the rnd

Scrap yarn for provisional cast on and holding stitches

Stitch markers

GAUGE

17 sts and 25 rnds = 4" / 10cm on larger needle in st st in the rnd.

14 sts and 32 rows = 4" / 10cm on larger needle in Fluffy Brioche Stitch worked flat.

SIZES

Finished chest circumference: 31[33½, 36, 38 ¼, 40½, 43] (45¼, 47½, 50, 52¼, 54½)" / 79[85, 91.5, 97, 103, 109.5] (115, 120.5, 127, 132.5, 138.5)cm.

Shown in size 36" with 1" / 2.5cm of negative ease.

Pippin

by Gudrun Johnston

SCHEMATIC

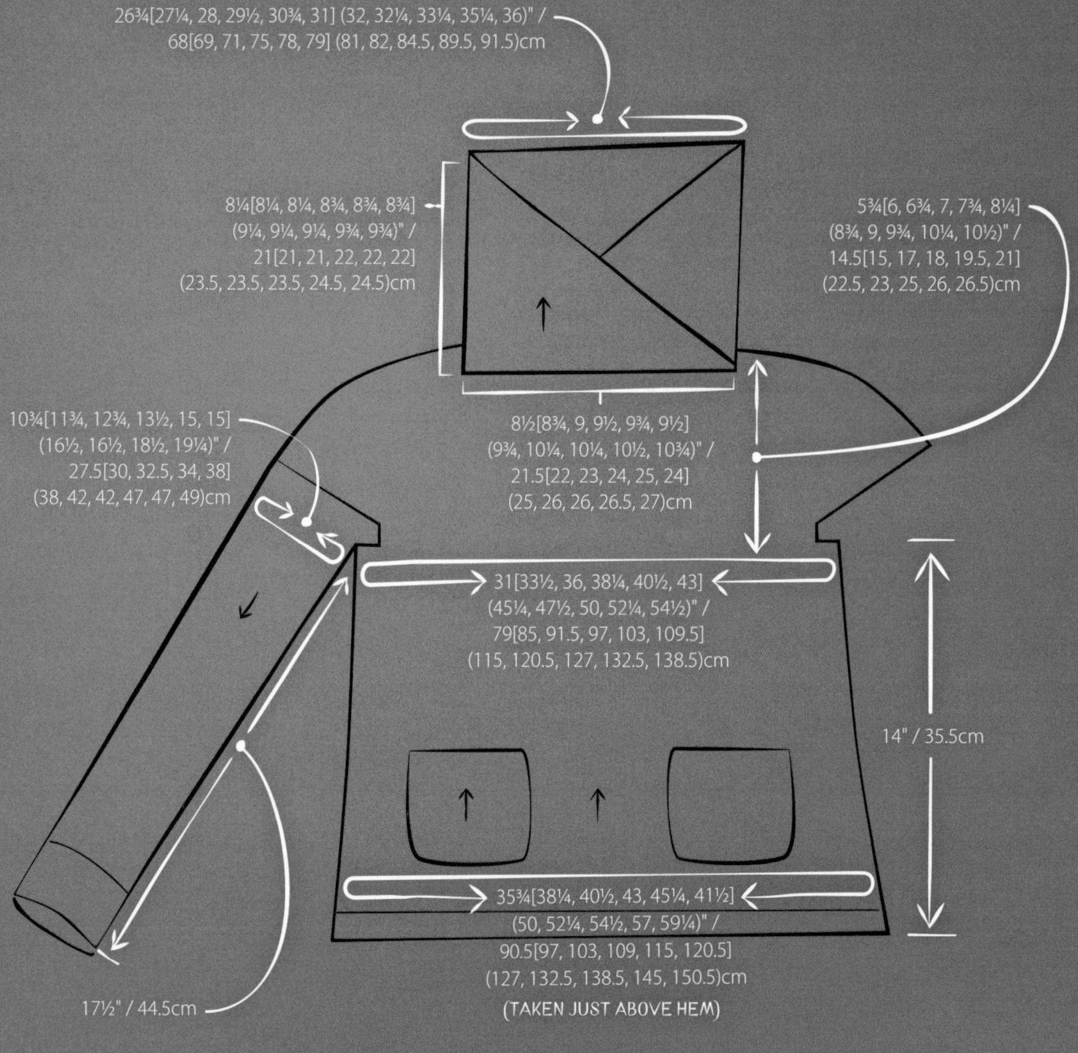

26¾[27¼, 28, 29½, 30¾, 31] (32, 32¼, 33¼, 35¼, 36)" /
68[69, 71, 75, 78, 79] (81, 82, 84.5, 89.5, 91.5)cm

8¼[8¼, 8¼, 8¾, 8¾, 8¾]
(9¼, 9¼, 9¼, 9¾, 9¾)" /
21[21, 21, 22, 22, 22]
(23.5, 23.5, 23.5, 24.5, 24.5)cm

5¾[6, 6¾, 7, 7¾, 8¼]
(8¾, 9, 9¾, 10¼, 10½)" /
14.5[15, 17, 18, 19.5, 21]
(22.5, 23, 25, 26, 26.5)cm

10¾[11¾, 12¾, 13½, 15, 15]
(16½, 16½, 18½, 19¼)" /
27.5[30, 32.5, 34, 38]
(38, 42, 42, 47, 47, 49)cm

8½[8¾, 9, 9½, 9¾, 9½]
(9¾, 10¼, 10¼, 10½, 10¾)" /
21.5[22, 23, 24, 25, 24]
(25, 26, 26, 26.5, 27)cm

31[33½, 36, 38¼, 40½, 43]
(45¼, 47½, 50, 52¼, 54½)" /
79[85, 91.5, 97, 103, 109.5]
(115, 120.5, 127, 132.5, 138.5)cm

14" / 35.5cm

17½" / 44.5cm

35¾[38¼, 40½, 43, 45¼, 41½]
(50, 52¼, 54½, 57, 59¼)" /
90.5[97, 103, 109, 115, 120.5]
(127, 132.5, 138.5, 145, 150.5)cm

(TAKEN JUST ABOVE HEM)

Stitch Pattern

FLUFFY BRIOCHE STITCH
worked flat

Begin with an even number of sts – note that your number of stitches will vary; count at the end of even rows. Note that first row is a WS row.

Row 1 (WS): *yo, sl 1 wyib, k1, rep from *.

Row 2: *k1, k2tog (the yo and sl st from previous row), rep from *.

Row 3: k1 * yo, sl 1 wyib, k1, rep from * to last st, k1.

Row 4: k2, *k2tog, k1; rep from *.

Directions

BODY

Using smaller needle, provisionally CO 152[162, 172, 182, 192, 202] (212, 222, 232, 242, 252) sts. Join rnd and pm to mark EOR.

K 7 rnds.

Next rnd (turning ridge): purl.

Change to larger needle, k 7 rnds.

Next rnd (joining rnd): undo provisional CO and slip resulting live sts onto smaller needle. Fold the hem at the purl ridge and hold the needles parallel so that the CO sts are behind the working sts. Knit each working st together with the corresponding CO st until all sts have been worked. 152[162, 172, 182, 192, 202] (212, 222, 232, 242, 252) sts.

Next rnd (place side marker): k76[81, 86, 91, 96, 101] (106, 111, 116, 121, 126), pm, knit to end.

K 3 rnds.

Next rnd — dec rnd: k1, k2tog, knit to 3 sts from side m, ssk, k1, sm, k1, k2tog, knit to 3 sts from end of rnd, ssk, k1.

K 15 rnds.

Rep last 16 rnds 3 more times.

Work dec rnd once more. 132[142, 152, 162, 172, 182] (192, 202, 212, 222, 232) sts.

K 9 rnds.

DIVIDE FOR FRONT AND BACK

Remove markers as you come to them.

Next rnd: k to 4[4, 5, 5, 5, 6] (6, 6, 7, 7, 7) sts from end of rnd. BO 8[8, 10, 10, 10, 12] (12, 12, 14, 14, 14) sts for underarm, k across 58[63, 66, 71, 76, 79] (84, 89, 92, 97, 102) back sts, BO 8[8, 10, 10, 10, 12] (12, 12, 14, 14, 14) sts for 2nd underarm, knit across 58[63, 66, 71, 76, 79] (84, 89, 92, 97, 102) front sts.

Place sts of back on hold to be worked later.

FRONT
Worked flat over 58[63, 66, 71, 76, 79] (84, 89, 92, 97, 102) sts rem on needles.

Beg with a WS row work 5 rows in st st.

Shape sleeve caps
Work following increases loosely so that the armhole edge doesn't pull in.

Row 1 (RS): k1, m1R, k to 1 st before end of row, m1L, k1. (2 sts inc).

Row 2: p1, m1p, p to 1 st before end of row, m1p, p1. (2 sts inc).

Rep last two rows 6[7, 7, 8, 9, 9] (9, 10, 10, 11, 12) more times. 86[95, 98, 107, 116, 119] (124, 133, 136, 145, 154) sts. **

Short rows

When directed to "turn," remember to prepare the work so that the gap can later be closed. Gudrun used the wrapless short row technique (see page 123) but other methods, such as wrap and turn, can be worked if preferred.

Row 1 (RS): k to 2 sts from end of row, turn.

Row 2: p to 2 sts from end of row, turn.

Row 3: k to 2 sts from previous gap, turn.

Row 4: p to 2 sts from previous gap, turn.

Rep last two rows 1[1, 2, 2, 3, 3] (3, 4, 4, 4, 4) more times.

Next Row (after last turn): k 19[23, 22, 25, 27, 29] (31, 33, 34, 38, 42) sts, join new yarn and BO 36[37, 38, 41, 42, 41] (42, 43, 44, 45, 46) sts, knit to 2 sts from previous gap, turn.

Shoulders are completed by working each side simultaneously with separate yarn. When directed to skip neck sts, drop yarn used for 1st shoulder and pick up yarn attached to 2nd shoulder.

Next Row (WS): p to bound off neck sts, skip neck sts, p to 2 sts from gap, turn.

Next Row: k to bound off neck sts, skip neck sts, k to 2 sts from gap, turn.

Next Row: p to bound off neck sts, skip neck sts, p to 2 sts from gap, turn.

Repeat last 2 rows 0[0, 0, 0, 1, 2] (2, 2, 2, 3, 3) more times.

Next Row: k to bound off neck sts, skip neck sts, k to 4[4, 5, 5, 5, 5] (5, 5, 5, 5, 5) sts from gap, turn.

Next Row (WS): p bound off neck sts, skip neck sts, p to 4[4, 5, 5, 5, 5] (5, 5, 5, 5, 5) sts from gap, turn.

Repeat last 2 rows 2[2, 2, 2, 2, 2] (3, 3, 3, 4, 4) more times.

There are 8[8, 9, 9, 11, 12] (13, 14, 14, 16, 16) turning points on each side.

Next Row: k to bound off neck sts, skip neck sts, k to end closing gaps on this shoulder as you come to them.

Next Row: p to bound off neck sts, skip neck sts, p to end closing gaps on this shoulder as you come to them.

Sl all sts to scrap yarn or stitch holders and break yarn.

BACK

Return held back sts to needles, with WS facing attach yarn and work as for front to **.

Short rows

Row 1 (RS): k to 2 sts from end of row, turn.

Row 2: p to 2 sts from end of row, turn.

Row 3: k to 2 sts from previous gap, turn.

Row 4: p to 2 sts from previous gap, turn.

Rep last 2 rows 3[3, 4, 4, 6, 7] (7, 8, 8, 9, 9) more times.

Next Row (RS): k to 4[4, 5, 5, 5, 5] (5, 5, 5, 5, 5) sts from gap, turn.

Next Row: p to 4[4, 5, 5, 5, 5] (5, 5, 5, 5, 5) sts from gap, turn.

Rep last 2 rows 2[2, 2, 2, 2, 2] (3, 3, 3, 4, 4) more times.

Next Row: k to end, closing gaps as you come to them.

Next Row: p25[29, 30, 33, 37, 39] (41, 45, 46, 50, 54), BO 36[37, 38, 41, 42, 41] (42, 43, 44, 45, 46) sts purlwise, p to end, closing gaps as you come to them.

Slip held front sts to spare smaller needle and Kitchener stitch front shoulder sts to back shoulder sts.

SLEEVES

Pick up sts around armhole using dpns or circulars for your preferred method. When picking up sts, you will pick up approx 1 st in each st on the underarm bind-offs, approx 3 sts per 4 rows on straight vertical edges and approx 1 st per row on diagonal sections as follows:

Beginning at centre of underarm sts, join yarn and pick up and knit 4[4, 5, 5, 6, 6] (7, 7, 8, 8, 8) underarm sts; pick up and knit 4[4, 5, 5, 5, 5] (5, 5, 6, 6, 6) sts on straight vertical edge; pick up and knit 15[17, 17, 19, 21, 21] (23, 23, 25, 25, 27) sts up diagonal edge of armhole; pick up and knit 15[17, 17, 19, 21, 21] (23, 23, 25, 25, 27) sts down 2nd diagonal edge; pick up and knit 4[4, 5, 5, 5, 5] (5, 5, 6, 6, 6) sts down 2nd straight edge; pick up and knit 4[4, 5, 5, 6, 6] (7, 7, 8, 8, 8) remaining underarm sts.

Place marker to mark end of rnd. 46[50, 54, 58, 64, 64] (70, 70, 78, 78, 82) sts.

*Next rnd — dec rnd: k1, k2tog, knit to last 3 sts, ssk, k1.

K 11[9, 7, 7, 7, 7] (5, 5, 5, 5, 5) rnds.

Rep from * 1[2, 3, 4, 5, 5] (5, 5, 6, 6, 8) more times. 42[44, 46, 48, 52, 52] (58, 58, 64, 64, 64) sts.

****Work dec rnd once more.

K 13[11, 11, 9, 9, 9] (7, 7, 7, 7, 7) rnds.

Rep from ** 0[0, 0, 0, 1, 1] (2, 2, 3, 3, 2) more times.

Work dec rnd once more. 38[40, 42, 44, 46, 46] (50, 50, 54, 54, 56) sts.

K 60[54, 48, 44, 36, 34] (32, 32, 18, 18, 14) more rnds, turn.

CUFF

Worked back and forth in rows.

Next row (WS): work row 1 of fluffy brioche stitch to end.

Work 25 more rows in fluffy brioche stitch, ending with row 2.

Bind off.

COWL
worked flat

Using smaller needle and beginning at bottom left hand corner of front neck with RS facing, join yarn and pick up and knit sts around neck as follows:

Pick up and knit 36[37, 38, 41, 42, 41] (42, 43, 44, 45, 46) in bound off front neck sts; pick up and knit 6 [6, 6, 6, 8, 9] (10, 10, 12, 14, 14] along vertical edge; pick up and knit 36[37, 38, 41, 42, 41] (42, 43, 44, 45, 46) across back neck; pick up and knit 6 [6, 6, 6, 8, 9] (10, 10, 12, 14, 14) down side of neck, and then, using Backward Loop cast-on, CO 36[37, 38, 41, 42, 41] (42, 43, 44, 45, 46) sts next to last picked up st. The number of sts picked up need not be precise, but must be an odd number; CO an extra st if necessary.

Change to larger needle and begin working back and forth in fluffy brioche stitch *as follows:*

Row 1 (WS): k1, (yo, sl 1 wyib, k1) to end.

Row 2: k3tog, (k1, k2tog) to last 4 sts (one of these is a yarn over from previous row), k3tog, k1. 2 sts dec.

Repeat last two rows 31[31, 31, 33, 33, 33] (35, 35, 35, 37, 37) more times. 64[64, 64, 68, 68, 68] (72, 72, 72, 76, 76) sts dec.

Work row 1 once more.

Work row 2 as written, binding off sts as they are worked.

POCKETS
worked flat

Using larger circular needle CO 18 sts.

Next row (WS): p1, work in fluffy brioche stitch to 1 st from end, p1.

Next row (RS): k1, work in fluffy brioche stitch to 1 st from end, k1.

Rep last 2 rows until a total of 6 repeats of fluffy brioche stitch have been worked (24 rows total).

Work 4 rows in st st.

Next Row (WS): k.

Work 2 more rows in st st

Next Row (RS): k4, k2tog, k5 k2tog, knit to end. 16 sts.

Purl one row.

Fold top of pocket over at the purl ridge and sew the live sts to the WS.

FINISHING

Sew the unattached edge of cowl along the inside of the front neck.

Sew the vertical edges of the cuffs together.

Weave in ends and block to match measurements shown.

Pin pockets in place to check for position, being sure that they are parallel to the hem and the same distance from the centre. Sew the bottom of the pockets to the body first, then the sides, being sure to sew the top corners securely in place before weaving in ends.

· · · · · · · ● · · · · · · ·

YARN

A soft worsted weight yarn with good stitch definition and elasticity; Cormo or Merino wool is ideal. Sample shown in Foxhill Farm 100% Cormo Wool (210yds/192m, 4oz/114g).

1000[1100, 1200] (1300, 1400, 1500, 1600) [1700] (1800, 1900, 2000, 2100)yds / 915[1005, 1100] (1190, 1280, 1310, 1460) [1555] (1695, 1740, 1830, 1920)m

NEEDLES AND NOTIONS

US 7 / 4.5mm 32" / 80cm or longer circular needle

US 7 / 4.5mm dpns or circulars for your preferred method of working small circumferences in the rnd

Two ½" / 12mm buttons

GAUGE

20 sts and 28 rnds = 4" / 10cm in st st in the rnd

22 sts and 28 rnds = 4" / 10cm in double seed stitch in the rnd

Sleeve cable = 1" / 2.5cm wide

Cable Panel Pattern = 12[13, 14, 15]" / 30[33, 35.5, 38]cm wide

SIZES

Finished chest circumference: 34[36, 38] (40, 42, 44, 46) [48] (50, 52, 54, 56)" / 86.5[91.5, 96.5] (101.5, 106.5, 112, 117) [122] (127, 132, 137, 142.25)cm

Shown in size 36" with 2" / 5cm of positive ease.

Note: If only 4 numbers are shown, follow the first number for sizes 34-38, the second for sizes 40-46, the third for size 48 only and the fourth for sizes 50-56.

Beekman Tavern

by Thea Colman

SCHEMATIC

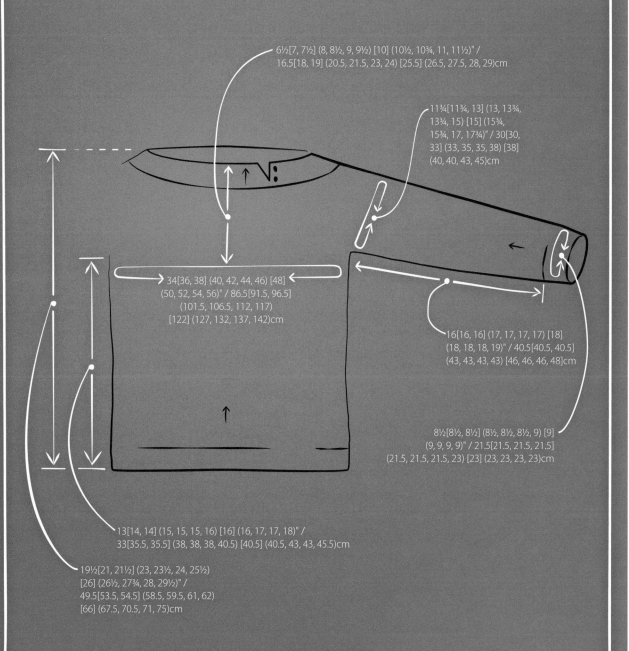

6½[7, 7½] (8, 8½, 9, 9½) [10] (10½, 10¾, 11, 11½)" /
16.5[18, 19] (20.5, 21.5, 23, 24) [25.5] (26.5, 27.5, 28, 29)cm

11¾[11¾, 13] (13, 13¾, 13¾, 15) [15] (15¾, 15¾, 17, 17¾)" / 30[30, 33] (33, 35, 35, 38) [38] (40, 40, 43, 45)cm

34[36, 38] (40, 42, 44, 46) [48] (50, 52, 54, 56)" / 86.5[91.5, 96.5] (101.5, 106.5, 112, 117) [122] (127, 132, 137, 142)cm

16[16, 16] (17, 17, 17, 17) [18] (18, 18, 18, 19)" / 40.5[40.5, 40.5] (43, 43, 43, 43) [46, 46, 46, 48]cm

8½[8½, 8½] (8½, 8½, 8½, 9) [9] (9, 9, 9, 9)" / 21.5[21.5, 21.5, 21.5] (21.5, 21.5, 21.5, 23) [23] (23, 23, 23, 23)cm

13[14, 14] (15, 15, 15, 16) [16] (16, 17, 17, 18)" /
33[35.5, 35.5] (38, 38, 38, 40.5) [40.5] (40.5, 43, 43, 45.5)cm

19½[21, 21½] (23, 23½, 24, 25½) [26] (26½, 27¾, 28, 29½)" /
49.5[53.5, 54.5] (58.5, 59.5, 61, 62) [66] (67.5, 70.5, 71, 75)cm

Stitch Patterns

CABLE PANEL PATTERN (FRONT AND BACK)

worked over a multiple of 5 sts in the rnd

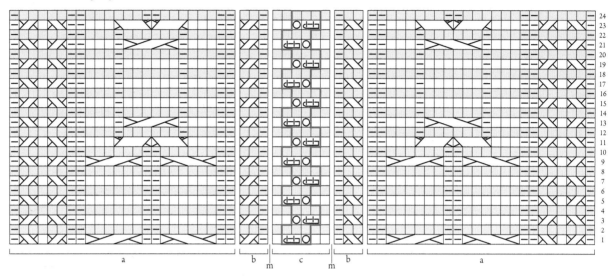

CHART NOTES

Work across full chart from right to left, repeating sections as follows:

a. work once.

b. work 1[1, 2, 2] time(s).

c. 27[33, 33, 39] sts between markers.

KEY

□	k	⤬ C6F	
−	p	⤬ C6B	
O	yo	⤬ C4F[p1, k3]	
⤡	C2B	⤢ C4B[k3, p1]	
⤢	C2F	□ repeat box	
d‐b	sl-k2-psso		

SLEEVE CABLE

Rnd 1: p1, C2B, k1, C2F, p1.

Rnd 2: p1, k5, p1.

Rnd 3: p1, C2F, k1, C2B, p1.

Rnd 4: rep rnd 2.

DOUBLE SEED STITCH

Rnds 1 and 2: k1, *(p1, k1) rep from * to end.

Rnds 3 and 4: p1, *(k1, p1) rep from * to end.

SPECIAL ABBREVIATIONS

sl1-k2-psso — slip 1, knit 2, pass the slipped stitch over the 2 knit stitches.

C4F[p1, k3] — slip 3 sts to cable needle and hold at front, p1, k3 sts from cable needle.

C4B[k3, p1] — slip 1 st to cable needle and hold at back, k3, p1 from cable needle.

C2B — sl1 st to cable needle and hold at back, k1, k1 st from the cable needle

C2F — sl1 st to cable needle and hold at front, k1, k1 st from the cable needle

C6B — slip 3 sts to cable needle and hold at back, k3, k3 sts from cable needle

C6F — slip 3 sts to cable needle and hold at front, k3, k3 sts from cable needle

CABLE PANEL PATTERN (FRONT AND BACK)
worked over a multiple of 5 sts in the rnd

Rnd 1: p1, C2B, k1, C2F, p2, C6F, p2, C6B, p2, (C2F, p1) 1[1, 2, 2] time(s), slm, k2, (yo, sl1-k2-psso) to 1 st before m, k1, slm, (p1, C2B) 1[1, 2, 2] time(s), p2, C6F, p2, C6B, p2, C2B, k1, C2F, p1.

Rnd 2: p1, k5, p2, (k6, p2) twice, (k2, p1) 1[1, 2, 2] time(s), slm, k to m, slm, (p1, k2) 1[1, 2, 2] time(s), (p2, k6) twice, p2, k5, p1.

Rnd 3: p1, C2F, k1, C2B, p2, (k6, p2) twice, (C2F, p1) 1[1, 2, 2] time(s), slm, k1, (sl1-k2-psso, yo) to 2 sts before m, k2, slm, (p1, C2B) 1[1, 2, 2] time(s), p2, (k6, p2) twice, C2F, k1, C2B, p1.

Rnds 4, 6, 8, 10: rep rnd 2.

Rnd 5: p1, C2B, k1, C2F, p2, (k6, p2) twice, (C2F, p1) 1[1, 2, 2] time(s), slm, k2, (yo, sl1-k2-psso) to 1 st before m, k1, slm, (p1, C2B) 1[1, 2, 2] time(s), (p2, k6) twice, p2, C2B, k1, C2F, p1.

Rnd 7: rep rnd 3.

Rnd 9: rep rnd 1.

Rnd 11: p1, C2F, k1, C2B, p2, k3, C4F[p1, k3], C4B[k3, p1], k3, p2, (C2F, p1) 1[1, 2, 2] time(s), slm, k1, (sl1-k2-psso, yo) to 2 sts before m, k2, slm, (p1, C2B) 1[1, 2, 2] time(s), p2, k3, C4F[p1, k3], C4B[k3, p1], k3, p2, C2F, k1, C2B, p1.

Rnd 12: p1, k5, p2, k3, p1, k6, p1, k3, p2, (k2, p1) 1[1, 2, 2] time(s), slm, k to m, slm, (p1, k2) 1[1, 2, 2] time(s), p2, k3, p1, k6, p1, k3, p2, k5, p1.

Rnd 13: p1, C2B, k1, C2F, p2, k3, p1, C6F, p1, k3, p2, (C2F, p1) 1[1, 2, 2] time(s), slm, k2, (yo, sl1-k2-psso) to 1 st before m, k1, slm, (p1, C2B) 1[1, 2, 2] time(s), p2, k3, p1, C6B, p1, k3, p2, C2B, k1, C2F, p1.

Rnds 14, 16, 18, 20, 22: rep rnd 12.

Rnd 15: p1, C2F, k1, C2B, p2, k3, p1, k6, p1, k3, p2, (C2F, p1) 1[1, 2, 2] time(s), slm, k1, (sl1-k2-psso, yo) to 2 sts before m, k2, slm, (p1, C2B) 1[1, 2, 2] time(s), p2, k3, p1, k6, p1, k3, p2, C2F, k1, C2B, p1.

Rnd 17: p1, C2B, k1, C2F, p2, k3, p1, k6, p1, k3, p2, (C2F, p1) 1[1, 2, 2] time(s), slm, k2, (yo, sl1-k2-psso) to 1 st before m, k1, slm, (p1, C2B) 1[1, 2, 2] time(s), p2, k3, p1, k6, p1, k3, p2, C2B, k1, C2F, p1.

Rnd 19: rep rnd 15.

Rnd 21: rep rnd 13.

Rnd 23: p1, C2F, k1, C2B, p2, k3, C4B[k3, p1], C4F[p1, k3], k3, p2, (C2F, p1) 1[1, 2, 2] time(s), slm, k1, (sl1-k2-psso, yo) to 2 sts before m, k2, slm, (p1, C2B) 1[1, 2, 2] time(s), p2, k3, C4B[k3, p1], C4F[p1, k3], k3, p2, C2F, k1, C2B, p1.

Rnd 24: p1, k5, (p2, k6) twice, p2, (k2, p1) 1[1, 2, 2] time(s), slm, k to m, slm, (p1, k2) 1[1, 2, 2] time(s), (p2, k6) twice, p2, k5, p1.

Directions

BODY

Using circular needle, CO 216[228, 240] (252, 264, 272, 284) [296] (308, 320, 332, 336) sts. For best results, use a cable cast-on for a defined edge.

Join rnd, place EOR marker.

Ribbing

Set up rnd: *k1, (p1, k1) 13[16, 19] (19, 22, 24, 27) [27] (27, 30, 33, 34) times, pm, (p1, k1) 3 times, (p2, k2) 5 times, p1, (k2, p1) 0[0, 1, 1] time(s), pm, k1, (p1, k1) 13[16, 16, 19] times, pm, p1, (k2, p1) 0[0, 1, 1] time(s), (k2, p2) 5 times, (k1, p1) 3 times*, pm, rep from * to * once.

Next rnd: work sts as they appear.

Next rnd: *k1, (p1, k1) to m, slm, (p1, k1) 3 times, (p2, k2) 4 times, p2, (C2F, p1) 1[1, 2, 2] time(s), slm, k1 (p1, k1) to m, slm, (p1, C2B) 1[1, 2, 2] times, p2, (k2, p2) 4 times, (k1, p1) 3 times*, slm, rep from * to * once more.

Next rnd: work sts as they appear.

Repeat the last 2 rounds 5 more times. Ribbing measures approximately 2" / 5cm.

Main body

Next rnd: *work in double seed stitch to m, slm, work next 81[87, 93, 99] sts in cable panel pattern*, slm, rep from * to * once.

Work even in patt as set, working sts on either side of cable panel pattern in double seed stitch as established and repeating rnds 1 – 24 of cable panel pattern, until body measures 13[14, 14] (15, 15, 15, 16) [16] (16, 17, 17, 18)" / 33[35.5, 35.5] (38, 38, 38, 40.5) [40.5] (40.5, 43, 43, 45.75)cm from cast on edge.

Next rnd: *work 11[14, 17] (17, 20, 22, 25) [25] (25, 28, 31, 32) sts in patt, bind off 5, work in patt to m, work cable panel pattern to m, rep from * once more. 103[109, 115] (121, 127, 131, 137) [143] (149, 155, 161,163) sts rem on front and back once divided.

Do not cut yarn.

SLEEVES — MAKE TWO

Using needles for your preferred method of working small circumferences in the rnd, CO 46[46, 46] (46, 46, 46, 50) [50] (50, 50, 50, 50) sts. For best results, use a cable cast-on for a defined edge.

Join rnd, pm to mark EOR.

Rnds 1 – 20: (p1, k1) to end.

Rnd 21: p1, k5, p1, k20[20, 20] (20, 20, 20, 25) [25] (25, 25, 25, 25) sts, pm, m1, k to end.

Next rnd: work rnd 1 of sleeve cable pattern over first 7 sts, k to end.

Continue to work first 7 sts in sleeve cable pattern throughout sleeve.

Work 7 rnds even.

*Next rnd — inc rnd: work in patt to 1 st before m, m1R, k1, slm, k1, m1L, k to end.

Work in patt for 11[11, 8] (8, 7, 6, 6) [6] (5, 5, 4, 4) rnds.

Rep from * 6[6, 9] (9, 11, 11, 12) [12] (14, 14, 17, 19) more times. 61[61, 67] (67, 71, 71, 77) [77] (81, 81, 87, 91) sts.

Work even in patt until sleeve measures 16[16, 16] (17, 17, 17, 17) [18] (18, 18, 18, 19)" / 40[40, 40] (43, 43, 43, 43) [46] (46, 46, 46, 48)cm from ribbing, or desired length.

Next rnd: work in patt to 2 sts before m; bind off 4, removing marker when you come to it; place rem sleeve sts on hold. Make a note of the last cable round worked. 57[57, 63] (63, 67, 67, 73) [73] (77, 77, 83, 87) sts.

YOKE

Joining sleeves and body

Next rnd: *work in patt across body to bound off sts, work in patt across sleeve, rep from * once more, place EOR marker (between sleeve and back). 320[332, 356] (368, 388, 396, 420) [432] (452, 464, 488, 500) sts.

Raglan shaping notes

The 'p1, k2, p1' between each set of markers forms the faux "seam" that defines the raglan shaping. Each k2 is worked with 1 st from the sleeve and 1 st from the body.

When directed to work in pattern, work each seam as 'p1, k2, p1' as established and maintain the double seed stitch and cable panels on body and sleeves as established. On non-decrease rounds always knit the first and last stitch before and after each "seam". When decreases affect the cable panel pattern work cables if there are enough stitches to do so; knit those stitches if there are not.

Next rnd: *k1, p1, pm, work in patt to 2 sts before join, pm, k1, p1, rep from * 3 more times.

Next rnd: *k1, p1, slm, k2tog, work in patt to 2 sts before m, ssk, slm, p1, k1, rep from * 3 more times.

Work 3 rnds in patt.

Rep last 4 rnds 0[1, 1] (1, 1, 1, 1) [2] (2, 2, 2, 3) more times.

Next rnd: *k1, p1, slm, k2tog, work in patt to 2 sts before m, ssk, slm, p1, k1, rep from * 3 more times.

Work 1 rnd in patt.

Rep last 2 rnds 17[17, 18](19, 21, 22, 24)[24](23, 26, 27, 27) more times. 19[17, 21] (19, 19, 17, 19) [17] (19, 17, 21, 23) sts on each sleeve, and 65[69, 73] (77, 79, 81, 83) [87] (91, 95, 99, 99) sts on front and back. 168[172, 788] (192, 196, 196, 204) [208] (220, 224, 240, 244) total sts.

Bind off.

FINISHING

Collar

Using circular needle, pick up and knit 5 sts for every 6 bound off sts around the neckline, beginning at the point just above the C2F to the side of the front central panel. Total st count must be an odd number, adjust if necessary.

Row 1 (RS): k1tbl, k1, (p1, k1) to 5 sts before end, p3, k1, k1tbl.

Row 2: sl1, p1, k3, (p1, k1) to 2 sts before end, p1, sl1.

Repeat these 2 rows 3 more times.

Work row 1 once more, adding 4 k2tog decreases, one above each seam; this will help the collar lie flat for a nice fit.

Next row: bind off in patt.

Weave in ends and block to measurements. Using sewing thread and needle, sew the two small buttons onto the purled panel on the collar, one above the other.

· · · · · · ● · · · · · ·

Pumpkin Ale

by Ysolda Teague

YARN

Worsted weight yarn with good elasticity and stitch definition, wool or wool blends are ideal.

Shown in Miss Babs Heartland Worsted (100% Merino, 250yds / 230m, 4oz / 115g) in Roasted Pumpkin.

920[960, 1040, 1120, 1150, 1250] (1310, 1400, 1440, 1510, 1610) [1680, 1750, 1840, 1900, 1960]yds / 840[880, 950, 1020, 1050, 1140] (1200, 1280, 1320, 1380, 1470) [1540, 1600, 1680, 1740, 1790]m.

NEEDLES AND NOTIONS

US 5 / 3.75mm 32" / 80cm or longer circular needle

US 5 / 3.75mm dpns or circulars for your preferred method of knitting small circumferences in the rnd

US 3 / 3.25mm 24" / 60cm or longer circular needle, for picking up sleeve stitches

Stitch markers

GAUGE

21 sts and 32 rows = 4"/10cm in st st.

SIZES

Finished chest circumference (with fronts overlapping): 30[32, 34, 36, 38, 40] (42, 44, 46, 48, 50) [52, 54, 56, 58, 60]" / 76[81.5, 86.5, 91.5, 96.5, 101.5] (106.5, 112, 117, 122, 127) [132, 137, 142, 147.5, 152.2]cm.

Shown in size 36" with 1" / 2.5cm of positive ease.

SCHEMATIC

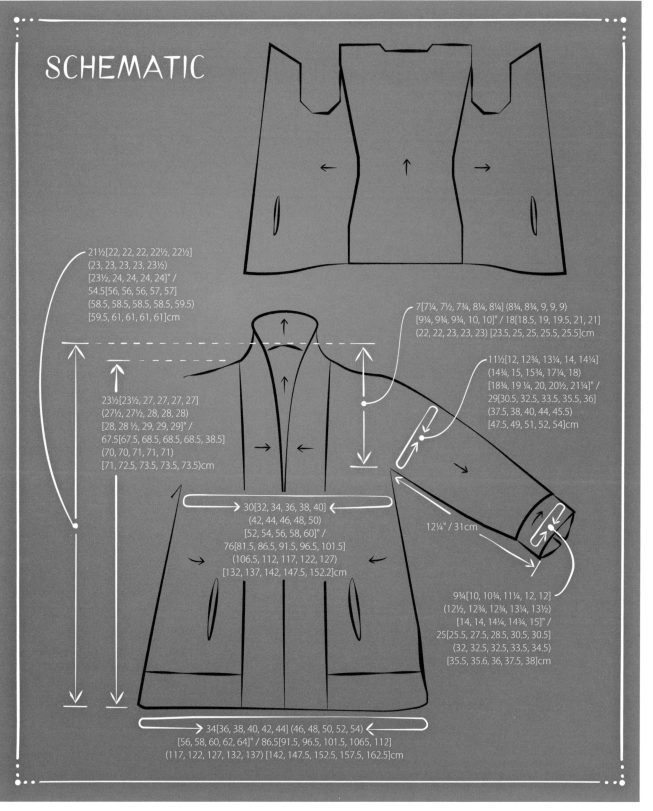

21½[22, 22, 22, 22½, 22½]
(23, 23, 23, 23, 23½)
[23½, 24, 24, 24, 24]" /
54.5[56, 56, 56, 57, 57]
(58.5, 58.5, 58.5, 58.5, 59.5)
[59.5, 61, 61, 61, 61]cm

7[7¼, 7½, 7¾, 8¼, 8¼] (8¾, 8¾, 9, 9, 9)
[9¼, 9¾, 9¾, 10, 10]" / 18[18.5, 19, 19.5, 21, 21]
(22, 22, 23, 23, 23) [23.5, 25, 25, 25.5, 25.5]cm

11½[12, 12¾, 13¼, 14, 14¼]
(14¾, 15, 15¾, 17¼, 18)
[18¾, 19 ¼, 20, 20½, 21¼]" /
29[30.5, 32.5, 33.5, 35.5, 36]
(37.5, 38, 40, 44, 45.5)
[47.5, 49, 51, 52, 54]cm

23½[23½, 27, 27, 27, 27]
(27½, 27½, 28, 28, 28)
[28, 28 ½, 29, 29, 29]" /
67.5[67.5, 68.5, 68.5, 68.5, 38.5]
(70, 70, 71, 71, 71)
[71, 72.5, 73.5, 73.5, 73.5]cm

30[32, 34, 36, 38, 40]
(42, 44, 46, 48, 50)
[52, 54, 56, 58, 60]" /
76[81.5, 86.5, 91.5, 96.5, 101.5]
(106.5, 112, 117, 122, 127)
[132, 137, 142, 147.5, 152.2]cm

12¼" / 31cm

9¾[10, 10¾, 11¼, 12, 12]
(12½, 12¾, 12¾, 13¼, 13½)
[14, 14, 14¼, 14¾, 15]" /
25[25.5, 27.5, 28.5, 30.5, 30.5]
(32, 32.5, 32.5, 33.5, 34.5)
[35.5, 35.6, 36, 37.5, 38]cm

34[36, 38, 40, 42, 44] (46, 48, 50, 52, 54)
[56, 58, 60, 62, 64]" / 86.5[91.5, 96.5, 101.5, 1065, 112]
(117, 122, 127, 132, 137) [142, 147.5, 152.5, 157.5, 162.5]cm

Stitch Patterns

RIGHT CABLE *worked over 14 sts*

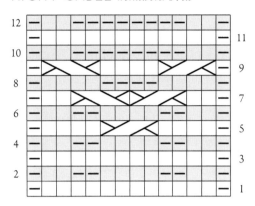

Row 1: p1, k12, p1.

Row 2: k1, p2, k2, p4, k2, p2, k1.

Rows 3–4: rep rows 1-2.

Row 5: p1, k4, C4B, k4, p1.

Row 6: rep row 2.

Row 7: p1, k2, C4B, C4F, k2, p1.

Row 8: k1, p4, k4, p4, k1.

Row 9: p1, C4B, k4, C4F, p1.

Row 10: k1, p2, k8, p2, k1.

Row 11: p1, k12, p1.

Row 12: rep row 10.

LEFT CABLE *worked over 14 sts*

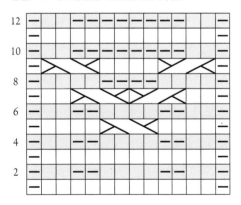

Rows 1–4: as for right cable.

Row 5: p1, k4, C4F, k4, p1.

Rows 6–12: as for right cable.

SLEEVE CABLE *worked over 10 sts*

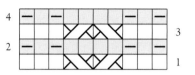

Row 1: k3, C2B, C2F, k3.

Row 2: k1, p1, k1, p4, k1, p1, k1.

Row 3: k3, C2F, C2B, k3.

Row 4: rep row 2.

After the sleeve caps are worked back and forth the sleeve cable will continue in the round. When working in the round work rounds 2 and 4 as follows: p1, k1, p1, k4, p1, k1, p1.

MINI CABLE *worked over 4 sts*

Row 1: C2B, C2F.

Row 2: p.

Row 3: C2F, C2B.

Row 4: p.

KEY

☐	k on rs, p on ws
—	p on rs, k on ws
⧄⧅	C2B — sl1 st to cable needle and hold at back, k1, k1 st from the cable needle
⧅⧄	C2F — sl1 st to cable needle and hold at front, k1, k1 st from the cable needle
⬡	C4B — slip 2 sts to cable needle and hold at back, k2, k2 sts from cable needle
⬡	C4F — slip 2 sts to cable needle and hold at front, k2, k2 sts from cable needle

Note

Short rows are used to shape the shoulders, waist and sleeve caps. When directed to 'turn', remember to prepare the work so that the gap can later be closed. Ysolda used the wrapless method (see page 123), but other methods can be worked if preferred.

Directions

BACK PANEL

Slip all stitches purlwise with yarn at wrong side of work.

CO 71[78, 78, 78, 85, 85] (85, 92, 92, 92, 99) [99, 99, 106, 106, 106] sts.

Row 1 (RS): sl2, k to end.

Row 2: sl2, k to 2 sts before end, p2.

Row 3: rep row 1.

Row 4: sl2, k4, (p4, k3) 2[2, 2, 2, 2, 2] (2, 3, 3, 3, 3) [3, 3, 3, 3, 3] times, pm, k1, p2, k8, p2, k1, pm, k3, (p4, k3) 0[1, 1, 1, 2, 2] (2, 1, 1, 1, 2) [2, 2, 3, 3, 3] times, pm, k1, p2, k8, p2, k1, pm, k3, (p4, k3) 2[2, 2, 2, 2, 2] (2, 3, 3, 3, 3) [3, 3, 3, 3, 3] times, k1, p2.

Row 5: sl2, k to m, slm, p1, k to 1 st before m, p1, slm, k to m, slm, p1, k to 1 st before m, p1, slm, k to end.

Row 6: sl2, k4, (p4, k3) to m, slm, k1, p2, k8, p2, k1, slm, k3, (p4, k3) to m, slm, k1, p2, k8, p2, k1, slm, k3, (p4, k3) to 3 sts from end, k1, p2.

Row 7 (RS): sl2, k4, (work row 1 of mini cable, k3) 2[2, 2, 2, 2, 2] (2, 3, 3, 3, 3) [3, 3, 3, 3, 3] times, slm, work row 1 of left cable, slm, k3, (work row1 of mini cable, k3) to m, slm, work row 1 of right cable, slm, k3, (work row 1 of mini cable, k3) 2[2, 2, 2, 2, 2] (2, 3, 3, 3, 3) [3, 3, 3, 3, 3] times, k3.

Work in patt as established in previous row, continuing to work 2-st wide I-cord borders and sts outside of cable patterns in garter st for 25 more rows (ending with row 2 of left and right cables).

Next row (RS): sl2, k2, k2tog, (work mini cable, k1, k2tog) 2[2, 2, 2, 2, 2] (2, 3, 3, 3, 3) [3, 3, 3, 3, 3] times, slm, work left cable, slm, k1, k2tog, (work mini cable, k1, k2tog) to m, slm, work right cable, slm, k1, k2tog, (work mini cable, k1, k2tog) 2[2, 2, 2, 2, 2] (2, 3, 3, 3, 3) [3, 3, 3, 3, 3] times, k3. 64[70, 70, 70, 76, 76] (76, 82, 82, 82, 88) [88, 88, 94, 94, 94] sts.

Work 27 rows in patt (ending with row 6 of left and right cables).

Next row (RS): sl2, k1, k2tog, (work mini cable, k2tog) 2[2, 2, 2, 2, 2] (2, 3, 3, 3, 3) [3, 3, 3, 3, 3] times, slm, work left cable, k2tog, (work mini cable, k2tog) to m, slm, work right cable, slm, k2tog, (work mini cable, k2tog) 2[2, 2, 2, 2, 2] (2, 3, 3, 3, 3) [3, 3, 3, 3, 3] times, k3. 57[62, 62, 62, 67, 67] (67, 72, 72, 72, 77) [77, 77, 82, 82, 82] sts.

Work 29 rows in patt (ending with row 12 of left and right cables).

Next row (RS): sl2, k1, kfb, (work mini cable, kfb) 2[2, 2, 2, 2, 2] (2, 3, 3, 3, 3) [3, 3, 3, 3, 3] times, slm, work left cable, kfb, (work mini cable, kfb) to m, slm, work right cable, slm, kfb, (work mini cable, kfb) 2[2, 2, 2, 2, 2] (2, 3, 3, 3, 3) [3, 3, 3, 3, 3] times, k3. 64[70, 70, 70, 76, 76] (76, 82, 82, 82, 88) [88, 88, 94, 94, 94] sts.

Work 45 rows in patt (ending with row 10 of left and right cables).

Next row (RS): sl2, k1, kfb, k1, (work mini cable, kfb, k1) 2[2, 2, 2, 2, 2] (2, 3, 3, 3, 3) [3, 3, 3, 3, 3] times, slm, work left cable, kfb, k1, (work mini cable, kfb, k1) to m, slm, work right cable, slm, kfb, k1, (work mini cable, kfb, k1) 2[2, 2, 2, 2, 2] (2, 3, 3, 3, 3) [3, 3, 3, 3, 3] times, k3. 71[78, 78, 78, 85, 85] (85, 92, 92, 92, 99) [99, 99, 106, 106, 106] sts.

Work 45 rows in patt (ending with row 8 of left and right cables).

Next row (RS): sl2, k2, kfb, k1, (work mini cable, k1, kfb, k1) 2[2, 2, 2, 2, 2] (2, 3, 3, 3, 3) [3, 3, 3, 3, 3] times, slm, work left cable, k1, kfb, k1, (work mini cable, k1, kfb, k1) to m, slm, work right cable, slm, k1, kfb, k1, (work mini cable, k1, kfb, k1) 2[2, 2, 2, 2, 2] (2, 3, 3, 3, 3) [3, 3, 3, 3, 3] times, k3. 78[86, 86, 86, 94, 94] (94, 102, 102, 102, 110) [110, 110, 118, 118, 118] sts.

Work 17[19, 21, 23, 27, 27] (29, 31, 33, 33, 35) [37, 39, 41, 41, 43] rows in patt.

Next row (RS): sl2, k20[22, 22, 22, 22, 22] (22, 24, 24, 24, 24) [24, 24, 26, 26, 26] bind off 34[38, 38, 38, 46, 46] (46, 50, 50, 50, 58) [58, 58, 58, 62, 62, 62], k to end.

Left shoulder — 22[24, 24, 24, 24, 24] (24, 26, 26, 26, 26) [26, 26, 28, 28, 28] sts.

Work left shoulder on sts just worked, leaving right shoulder sts on needles.

Next row (WS): sl2, k to end.

Next row: k1, ssk, k to end.

Rep last 2 rows once more.

Next row: sl2, k to end.

Bind off.

Right shoulder — 22[24, 24, 24, 24, 24] (24, 26, 26, 26, 26) [26, 26, 28, 28, 28] *sts.*

Join yarn at neck edge of right shoulder sts.

Next row (WS): k to 2 sts before end, p2.

Next row: sl2, k to 3 sts before end, k2tog, k1.

Rep last 2 rows once more.

Next row: k to 2 sts before end, p2.

Bind off.

RIGHT SIDE PANEL

Beginning at right bottom corner of back panel and working up from the cast on edge, insert needle under strands across back of I-cord until 78[78, 79, 80, 80, 80] (81, 81, 82, 83, 83) [84, 85, 85, 85, 86) strands have been picked up along vertical edge to the underarm. The remaining sts will create the back of the armhole. Slide picked up loops along needle so that left tip is at bottom corner and join yarn with right side facing.

Row 1 (RS): (k4, kfb) to 3[3, 4, 5, 5, 0] (1, 1, 2, 3, 3) [4, 5, 5, 0, 1] sts before end, k to end. 93[93, 94, 95, 95, 96] (97, 97, 98, 99, 99) [100, 101, 101, 102, 103] sts.

Row 2 (WS): p to 16 sts before end, pm for border, (k1, p3) twice, (k1, p1) twice, k3, p1.

When directed to work in pattern, k all sts on RS rows and work WS rows as established in row 2. Sl the first st of every RS row.

Armhole decreases and waist increases

Next row — dec row (RS): sl1, k to 3 sts before end, k2tog, k1.

Next row: work in patt.

Rep the last two rows 0[0, 0, 0, 0, 1] (1, 1, 1, 2, 2) [2, 2, 2, 3, 3] more times.

Next row (RS): sl1, k to m, k27, m1, pm for waist, (k2, m1) 5 times, k to 3 sts before end, k2tog, k1.

Next row: work in patt.

Decreasing at the end of each RS row as established in initial dec row work 0[0, 2, 2, 2, 2] (4, 4, 4, 4, 4) [6, 6, 6, 6, 8] rows in patt.

Next row (RS): sl1, k to waist m, remove m, m1, (k3, m1) 5 times, k to 3 sts before end, k2tog, k1.

Next row: work in patt.

Decreasing at the end of each RS row as established in initial dec row work 0[0, 0, 2, 2, 2] (2, 2, 4, 4, 4) [4, 6, 6, 6, 6] rows in patt.

Waist short rows

Work 2[2, 4, 6, 6, 8] (10, 10, 12, 14, 14) [16, 18, 18, 20, 22] rows in patt ending with a WS row.

Next row (RS): sl1, k to border m, slm, k3, turn.

Next row: work in patt to end.

Next row: sl1, k to gap, pm, close gap, k18, turn.

Next row: work in patt to end.

Rep last two rows twice.

Next row: sl1, k to gap, pm, close gap, k to end.

Work 3 rows in patt.

Next row (RS): sl1, k to m closest to underarm edge, remove m, turn.

Next row: work in patt to end.

Rep last two rows 3 more times.

Next row: sl1, k to end, closing gaps as you come to them.

Work 3[3, 5, 7, 7, 9] (11, 11, 13, 15, 15) [17, 19, 19, 21, 23] rows in patt ending with a WS row.

Armhole increases

Next row: sl 1, k to 2 sts before end, m1L, k2.

Next row: work in patt.

Rep last 2 rows 2[2, 3, 4, 4, 5] (6, 6, 7, 8, 8) [9, 10, 10, 11, 12] more times. 105[105, 106, 107, 107, 108] (109, 109, 110, 111, 111) [112, 113, 113, 114, 115] sts.

Pocket set-up and armhole cast-on

Prepare for pocket by provisionally casting on 30 sts using a spare needle and waste yarn. Set aside.

Next row (RS): sl1, k to end, then using working yarn and needles, cable cast on 22 sts for the front of the armhole.

Next row: p to border marker, slm, work in patt to end.

Next row: work in patt to border m, slm, k4, put next 30 sts on hold, k across provisionally cast on sts, k to end.

Next row: work in patt to end.

Shoulder shaping

Next row: sl1, k to 2 sts before end, m1L, k2.

Next row: work in patt to end.

Rep last 2 rows 11[12, 12, 12, 12, 12] (12, 13, 13, 13, 13) [13, 13, 15, 15, 15] more times. 139[140, 141, 142, 142, 143] (144, 145, 146, 147, 147) [148, 149, 151, 152, 153]sts.

Slip all sts onto scrap yarn.

LEFT SIDE PANEL

Beginning at left bottom corner of back panel insert needle under strands across back of I-cord until 78[78, 79, 80, 80, 80] (81, 81, 82, 83, 83)[84, 85, 85, 85, 86] strands have been picked up along vertical edge. Remaining sts will create the back of the armhole. With RS facing join yarn at last strand picked up at armhole edge.

Row 1 (RS): (k4, kfb) to 3[3, 4, 5, 5, 0] (1, 1, 2, 3, 3) [4, 5, 5, 0, 1] sts before end, k to end. 93[93, 94, 95, 95, 96] (97, 97, 98, 99, 99) [100, 101, 101, 102, 103] sts.

Row 2 (WS): sl1, k3, (p1, k1) twice, (p3, k1) twice, pm, p to end.

Armhole decreases and waist increases

Next row — dec row (RS): k1, ssk, k to end.

Next row: work in patt as for row 2.

Rep the last 2 rows 0[0, 0, 0, 0, 1] (1, 1, 1, 2, 2) [2, 2, 2, 3, 3] more times.

Next row (RS): k1, ssk, k to 37 sts before m, m1, pm for waist, (k2, m1) 5 times, k to end.

Next row: work in patt.

Decreasing at the beg of each RS row as established in initial dec row work 0[0, 0, 2, 2, 2](4, 4, 4, 4, 4)[6, 6, 6, 6, 8] rows in patt.

Next row (RS): k1, ssk, k to waist m, remove m, m1, (k3, m1) 5 times, k to end.

Next row: work in patt.

Decreasing at the beg of each RS row as established in initial dec row work 0[0, 0, 2, 2, 2](2, 2, 4, 4, 4)[4, 6, 6, 6, 6] rows in patt. 102 sts.

Waist short rows

Work 3[3, 5, 7, 7, 9] (11, 11, 13, 15, 15) [17, 19, 19, 21, 23] rows in patt ending with a RS row.

Next row (WS): work in patt to border m, slm, p3, turn.

Next row: k to end.

Next row: work in patt to gap, pm, close gap, p18, turn.

Next row: k to end.

Rep last two rows twice.

Next row: work in patt to gap, pm, close gap, p to end.

Work 3 rows in patt.

Next row: work in patt to m closest to underarm edge, remove m, turn.

Next row: k to end.

Rep last two rows 3 more times.

Next row: work in patt to border m, slm, p to end closing gaps as you come to them.

Work 2[2, 4, 6, 6, 8] (10, 10, 12, 14, 14) [16, 18, 18, 20, 22] rows in patt.

Armhole increases

Next row: k2, m1R, k to end.

Next row: work in patt.

Rep last 2 rows 2[2, 3, 4, 4, 5] (6, 6, 7, 8, 8) [9, 10, 10, 11, 12] more times. 105[105, 106, 107, 107, 108] (109, 109, 110, 111, 111) [112, 113, 113, 114, 115] sts.

Pocket set-up and armhole cast on

Prepare for pocket by provisionally casting on 30 sts with spare needle and scrap yarn. Set aside.

Next row (RS): k.

Next row: work in patt to end, use working needles and yarn to cable cast on 22 sts for the front of the armhole.

Next row: k to end.

Next row: work in patt to border m, slm, p4, put next 30 sts on hold, p across provisionally cast on sts, p to end.

Shoulder shaping

Next row: k2, m1R, k to end.

Next row: work in patt to end.

Rep last 2 rows 11[12, 12, 12, 12, 12] (12, 13, 13, 13, 13) [13, 13, 15, 15, 15] more times. 139[140, 141, 142, 142, 143] (144, 145, 146, 147, 147) [148, 149, 151, 152, 153] sts.

Slip all sts onto scrap yarn.

SLEEVES

Before working sleeves join shoulder seams.

Setting up right sleeve

On back panel count down 16[18, 18, 18, 20, 20] (20, 20, 20, 20, 20) [20, 22, 22, 22, 22] garter ridges from the shoulder seam and use a safety pin to mark the edge of the right armhole at this point.

Beginning at the marked point, with RS facing, join yarn and using smaller needles pick up and knit sts around armhole as follows (picking up sts from I-cord edge as for side panels):

13[14, 14, 14, 15, 15] (15, 15, 15, 15, 15) [15, 16, 16, 16, 16] sts to shoulder seam, 20[20, 20, 20, 21, 21] (21, 22, 22, 25, 27) [28, 28, 29, 29, 30] sts down front of armhole to straight edge of underarm, 5[5, 9, 11, 11, 13] (15, 15, 19, 21, 21) [23, 23, 25, 27, 29] sts across underarm, 23[24, 24, 24, 26, 26] (26, 27, 27, 30, 32) [33, 34, 35, 35, 36] sts up back of armhole to marked point. 61[63, 67, 69, 73, 75] (77, 79, 83, 91, 95) [99, 101, 105, 107, 111] sts.

Setting up left sleeve

On back panel count down 4[5, 5, 5, 6, 6] (6, 6, 6, 6, 6) [6, 7, 7, 7, 7] garter ridges from the shoulder seam and use a safety pin to mark the edge of the left armhole at this point.

Beginning at the marked point join yarn and using smaller needles pick up and knit sts around armhole as follows: 33[34, 34, 34, 36, 36] (36, 37, 37, 40, 42) [43, 44, 45, 45, 46] sts down back of armhole to straight edge of underarm, 5[5, 9, 11, 11, 13] (15, 15, 19, 21, 21) [23, 23, 25, 27, 29] sts across underarm, 20[20, 20, 20, 21, 21] (21, 22, 22, 25, 27) [28, 28, 29, 29, 30] sts up front of armhole to shoulder seam, 3[4, 4, 4, 5, 5] (5, 5, 5, 5, 5) [5, 6, 6, 6, 6] sts to marked point.

Sleeve cap
work both the same

The sleeve cap is shaped with short rows and should be worked back and forth beginning at the marked point with the right side facing. Work sleeve cap with larger circular needle, leaving picked up stitches resting on smaller needles until they are incorporated as the short rows get longer and longer. When the sleeve cap is complete the sleeve will be worked in rounds with the beginning of the round at the underarm.

Row 1 (RS): k14 sts, turn.

Next row: p4, pm, work 10 sts in sleeve cable pattern beginning with Row 1, pm, p4, turn.

You will continue to work the 10 sts between markers in sleeve cable pattern and all other stitches in stockinette as established.

Next row: work in patt to gap, close gap, k3, turn.

Next row: work in patt to gap, close gap, p3, turn.

Rep last 2 rows 0[0, 0, 0, 1, 1] (1, 1, 1, 1, 1) [1, 1, 1, 1, 1] more times.

Whichever short row method is used closing the gap on the following rows must involve working one stitch from the initial pick up round: each turn will therefore be worked 1 st beyond the previous one.

Next row (RS): work in patt to gap, close gap, turn.

Next row: work in patt to gap, close gap, turn.

Rep last 2 rows 14[15, 15, 15, 13, 13] (13, 14, 14, 17, 19) [20, 21, 22, 22, 23] more times.

Next row: k to gap, close gap, k2[2, 4, 5, 5, 6] (7, 7, 9, 10, 10) [11, 11, 12, 13, 14], pm to mark EOR, and distribute sts evenly over needles for working small circumferences in the rnd. 61[63, 67, 69, 73, 75] (77, 79, 83, 91, 95) [99, 101, 105, 107, 111] sts.

Sleeves

Next rnd: p1, work in patt to gap, close gap, k to end.

Work the rest of the sleeve purling the first st of rnd on alternate rnds, maintaining sleeve cable pattern as established, and knitting all other sts, following the shaping directions below.

**Work 11[11, 11, 11, 11, 10] (10, 10, 10, 7, 5) [4, 4, 4, 3, 3] rnds even.

Next rnd: work 1 st, ssk, work in patt to 3 sts from end, k2tog, k1.

Rep from ** 4[4, 4, 4, 4, 5] (5, 5, 7, 10, 11) [12, 13, 14, 14, 15] more times. 51[53, 57, 59, 63, 63] (65, 67, 67, 69, 71) [73, 73, 75, 77, 79] sts.

Work 11[11, 11, 11, 11, 5] (5, 5, 7, 5, 11) [6, 1, 11, 11, 7] rnds even.

Right sleeve only: work 2 rnds in patt removing markers on last rnd and stopping 7 sts before sleeve cable panel. Break yarn and set sleeve aside leaving sts on needles.

Left sleeve only: work next rnd in patt removing all markers; k 6 sts past the cable panel. Break yarn and set sleeve aside leaving sts on needles or holder if necessary.

CUFF

With larger circular needle, cast on 17 sts. Cuff is worked back and forth and joined to the live stitches of the sleeve at the end of each RS row.

Row 1 (RS): sl1, k to 1 st from end, ssk (joining 1 st from cuff to 1 st from sleeve).

Row 2: sl1, (k1, p3) twice, (k1, p1) twice, k3, p1.

Row 3: sl1, k to 1 st from end, sssk (joining 1 st from cuff to 2 sts from sleeve).

Row 4: rep row 2.

Rep rows 1–4 until either 1, 2 or 3 live sts remain. If 1 st remains work row 1 once more, if 2 sts remain work row 3 once more, if 3 sts rem work rows 1–3 once more.

Bind off knitwise from WS.

FRONT BORDER

Return held stitches for right and then left front to larger circular.

Beginning at bottom edge of right front: sl1, k right front sts; pick up and knit sts across back neck, picking up 4 sts along each diagonal edge and 1 st for every stitch across bound-off edge; k to end.

Slipping 1st st of every row work 33[37, 37, 37, 41, 43] (43, 47, 47, 47, 55) [55, 55, 57, 57, 57] rows in garter st beg and ending with a WS row.

Work I-cord bind off as follows: with RS facing cable cast on 2 sts next to first stitch, *k2, ssk, slip 3 sts just worked back to left needle tip, rep from * until all stitches from front border have been bound off. Break yarn and draw through rem 3 sts.

POCKET EDGE — MAKE TWO

Return held sts for pocket to needles for working small circumferences in the round. Join yarn and knit across these sts; cable cast on 7 sts next to sts just worked; remove provisional cast on and slip resulting live sts onto left needle; knit across these sts; cable cast on 7 sts next to sts just worked; join rnd. 74 sts.

Next rnd: k33, p1, k36, p1, k3.

Rep last rnd 4 more times. Bind off.

FINISHING

Turn pocket edges to inside and sew up small holes on either side. Weave in ends. Block to measurements shown.

POCKET LININGS

Fold fabric right sides together and cut around pocket template, on page 180, twice (4 pieces). Finish straight edges in a way appropriate for your fabric (zig-zag, pinking, etc.) With right sides together sew pairs together around curved edge and finish seam allowance, bias binding makes a particularly neat finish. Turn pocket inside out and, with wrong sides facing insert pocket through hole in sweater so that fabric extends approx. ¼" beyond bind off edge. Take care to

line up seams on pocket with knit stitches on pocket edge, fold seam allowances from sides of pocket to one side and stitch all around opening. With right side facing push pocket to inside and press fabric edges. Slipstitch bottom of pocket to border of cardigan on the inside so that pockets don't droop.

· · · · · · · ● · · · · · ·

Aunt Fred

by Pamela Wynne

YARN

Non-superwash wool yarn. Briar Rose Nate's Yarn (100% wool, 500yds / 457m, 4.94oz / 140g) shown in MC: Old Gold, and CC: Undyed.

MC: 700[750, 800, 850, 900, 900] (950, 1000, 1000, 1050, 1100) [1150, 1200, 1250, 1300, 1300]yds / 700[750, 750, 800, 850, 900] (950, 950, 1000, 1000, 1050) [1100, 1150, 1200, 1250, 1250]m

CC: 500[550, 550, 600, 600, 650] (650, 700, 700, 750, 750) [800, 850, 850, 900, 900]yds / 450[500, 550, 550, 600, 600] (650, 650, 700, 750, 750) [800, 800, 800, 850, 850]m

NEEDLES AND NOTIONS

US 5 / 3.75 mm 24" /60cm circular needle and dpns or needles for your preferred method or working small circumferences in the rnd.

US 3 / 3.25 mm 24"/60cm circular needle and dpns or needles for your preferred method or working small circumferences in the rnd.

Additionally, for sizes 42 – 50" a 32" / 80cm length, and for sizes 52 – 60" a 40"/100cm length circular in the same size. For these sizes, begin with the longest needle and switch to a shorter needle as desired while working the yoke.

GAUGE

24 sts and 28 rnds = 4" / 10 cm in stranded colourwork patt worked in the rnd with larger needle, after blocking.

Note: soak swatch to test for excess dye bleeding from dyed to un-dyed yarn. Wash finished garment carefully in cold water with a gentle wool wash and ideally steam block to help prevent future dye bleed.

SIZES

Finished chest circumference: 30[32, 34, 36, 38, 40] (42, 44, 46, 48, 50) [52, 54, 56, 58, 60]" / 76[81.5, 86.5, 91.5, 96.5, 101.5] (106.5, 112, 117, 122, 127) [132, 137, 142, 147.5, 152.5]cm.

Shown in size 30" with zero ease.

SCHEMATIC

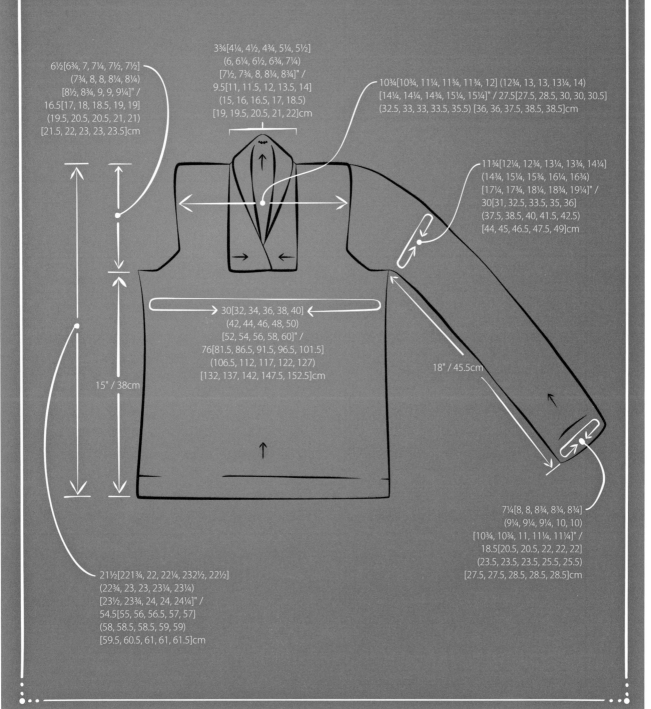

6½[6¾, 7, 7¼, 7½, 7½]
(7¾, 8, 8, 8¼, 8¼)
[8½, 8¾, 9, 9, 9¼]" /
16.5[17, 18, 18.5, 19, 19]
(19.5, 20.5, 20.5, 21, 21)
[21.5, 22, 23, 23, 23.5]cm

3¾[4¼, 4½, 4¾, 5¼, 5½]
(6, 6¼, 6½, 6¾, 7¼)
[7½, 7¾, 8, 8¼, 8¾]" /
9.5[11, 11.5, 12, 13.5, 14]
(15, 16, 16.5, 17, 18.5)
[19, 19.5, 20.5, 21, 22]cm

10¾[10¾, 11¼, 11¾, 11¾, 12] (12¾, 13, 13, 13¼, 14)
[14¼, 14¼, 14¾, 15¼, 15¼]" / 27.5[27.5, 28.5, 30, 30, 30.5]
(32.5, 33, 33, 33.5, 35.5) [36, 36, 37.5, 38.5, 38.5]cm

11¾[12¼, 12¾, 13¼, 13¾, 14¼]
(14¾, 15¼, 15¾, 16¼, 16¾)
[17¼, 17¾, 18¼, 18¾, 19¼]" /
30[31, 32.5, 33.5, 35, 36]
(37.5, 38.5, 40, 41.5, 42.5)
[44, 45, 46.5, 47.5, 49]cm

30[32, 34, 36, 38, 40]
(42, 44, 46, 48, 50)
[52, 54, 56, 58, 60]" /
76[81.5, 86.5, 91.5, 96.5, 101.5]
(106.5, 112, 117, 122, 127)
[132, 137, 142, 147.5, 152.5]cm

15" / 38cm

18" / 45.5cm

21½[22¾, 22, 22¼, 23½, 22½]
(22¾, 23, 23, 23¼, 23¼)
[23½, 23¾, 24, 24, 24¼]" /
54.5[55, 56, 56.5, 57, 57]
(58, 58.5, 58.5, 59, 59)
[59.5, 60.5, 61, 61, 61.5]cm

7¼[8, 8, 8¾, 8¾, 8¾]
(9¼, 9¼, 9¼, 10, 10)
[10¾, 10¾, 11, 11¼, 11¼]" /
18.5[20.5, 20.5, 22, 22, 22]
(23.5, 23.5, 23.5, 25.5, 25.5)
[27.5, 27.5, 28.5, 28.5, 28.5]cm

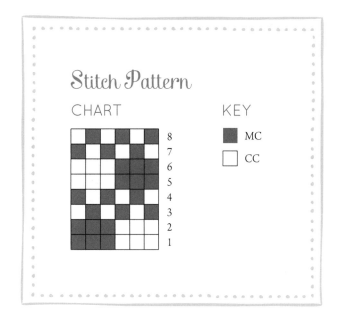

Stitch Pattern

CHART

KEY

■ MC

□ CC

Directions

BODY

With MC, using smaller circular needle CO 180[192, 204, 216, 228, 240] (252, 264, 276, 288, 300) [312, 324, 336, 348, 360] sts. For best results use a tubular cast on for 2x2 rib (see page 154). Join rnd and pm to mark end of rnd.

Work in 2x2 rib (k2, p2) until piece measures 2.5" / 6.5cm from cast-on edge.

Change to larger circular needle, join CC, and begin working from chart. Continue to work in patt until body piece measures 15" / 38cm from cast-on edge, or desired length from hip to underarm, ending with row 4 or 8. Set body piece aside. Make note of last chart row completed.

SLEEVES — MAKE TWO

With MC, using smaller dpns (or preferred needles for working small circumferences in the rnd) CO 44[48, 48, 52, 52, 52] (56, 56, 56, 60, 60) [64, 64, 68, 68, 68] sts. For best results use a tubular cast on for 2x2 rib. Join rnd and pm to mark end of rnd.

Work in 2x2 rib (k2, p2) until piece measures 2.5" / 6.5cm from cast-on edge.

Next rnd: change to larger needle, m1 in MC (seam st), join CC, pm, and work rem sts using row 1 of colour chart. Always work seam st in MC. Continue working charted patt in the rnd.

Note: Chart will not rep an even number of times around the sts of the sleeve; incorporate new sts into the charted patt as they are increased.

Work 7 rnds in patt, maintaining seam st in MC.

*Next rnd — inc rnd: k seam st, slm, m1, work in charted patt to end of rnd, m1. 2 sts increased.

Work 6[7, 6, 6, 5, 5] (5, 4, 4, 4, 4) [4, 3, 4, 3, 3] rnds even.

Rep from * 12[11, 13, 12, 14, 15] (15, 16, 18, 17, 19) [18, 20, 19, 21, 22] more times. 71[73, 77, 79, 83, 85] (89, 91, 95, 97, 101) [103, 107, 109, 113, 115] sleeve sts (including seam st).

Continue to work in patt until sleeve measures 18" / 46cm from cast-on edge, or desired length from wrist to underarm, ending with row 4 or row 8. On final rnd, work in patt to 4[5, 5, 6, 7, 8] (8, 9, 10, 11, 11) [12, 13, 14, 14, 15] sts from end.

Slip next 8[10, 10, 12, 14, 16] (16, 18, 20, 22, 22) [24, 26, 28, 28, 30] sts onto scrap yarn for underarm. Put remaining 63[63, 67, 67, 69, 69] (73, 73, 75, 75, 79) [79, 81, 81, 85, 85] sts on hold.

YOKE

Return to held stitches for body.

Continuing with larger circular needle, beginning at the next st of the body, *k1 in MC (seam st), work 80[84, 90, 94, 98, 102] (108, 112, 116, 120, 126) [130, 134, 138, 144, 148] sts in patt as established, k1 in MC (seam st), pm, slip next 8[10, 10, 12, 14, 16] (16, 18, 20, 22, 22) [24, 26, 28, 28, 30] sts onto waste yarn for underarm, work live sts of sleeve maintaining sleeve patt as established, pm, rep from * once more.

290[298, 318, 326, 338, 346] (366, 374, 386, 394, 414) [422, 434, 442, 462, 470] total sts for yoke.

Next rnd (body dec rnd — work all decs using MC): *ssk, k to 2 sts before marker, k2tog, slm, k to m, slm, rep from * once more.

Rep body dec rnd 3 more times.

SET UP COLLAR STEEK

Next rnd: ssk with MC, work 23[25, 27, 29, 31, 33] (36, 37, 39, 41, 43) [45, 46, 48, 50, 52] sts in patt, place 24[24, 26, 26, 26, 26] (26, 28, 28, 28, 30) [30, 32, 32, 34, 34] sts at centre front on waste yarn, pm, cast on 7 sts for steek, pm, k to 2 sts before marker, k2tog with MC, slm, k to m, slm, ssk with MC, k to 2 sts before marker, k2tog with MC, slm, k to end.

On subsequent rnds, when you reach the steek sts, work them in a vertical stripe patt, alternating between MC and CC.

Rep body dec rnd: 3[5, 6, 7, 9, 10] (11, 12, 14, 15, 16) [17, 19, 20, 21, 23] more times.

66[66, 70, 72, 72, 74] (78, 80, 80, 82, 86) [88, 88, 90, 94, 94] sts remain between markers for back.

Next rnd (sleeve dec set up rnd): working all decs in MC, remove marker, k seam stitch in MC, pm to mark new end of rnd, k to 1 st before m, pm, ssk (working seam st together with first st of sleeve and removing marker), k to 1 st before marker, k2tog, (working seam st together with last st of sleeve and removing marker), pm, k to 1 st before m, pm, ssk (working seam st together with first st of sleeve and removing marker), k to 2 sts before end, k2tog.

Next rnd: work in patt as established, maintaining seam sts in MC.

Next rnd (sleeve dec rnd): working decs with MC, *k to m, slm, ssk, k to 2 sts before marker, k2tog, slm, rep from * once more.

Next rnd: work in patt as established, maintaining seam sts in MC.

Rep last two rnds 9[11, 11, 11, 12, 12] (12, 14, 12, 12, 12) [14, 15, 14, 14, 14] more times — 43[39, 43, 43, 43, 43] (47, 45, 49, 49, 53) [49, 49, 51, 55, 55] sleeve sts remain between markers.

Rep sleeve dec rnd only 17[15, 17, 17, 17, 17] (19, 17, 19, 19, 21) [19, 19, 19, 21, 21] more times — 11[11, 11, 11, 11, 11] (11, 13, 13, 13, 13) [13, 13, 15, 15, 15] sleeve sts remain between markers.

Front shoulders

Worked back and forth on front stitches, consuming remaining sleeve stitches with a decrease at the end of each row.

Next row: sl1, k across front sts including steek, maintaining patt, to second (right front) seam st, with MC, ssk (the seam st and 1 sleeve st), turn.

Next row (WS): sl1, p across front sts including steek, maintaining patt, to left front seam st, with MC, p2tog (the seam st and 1 sleeve st), turn.

Rep last 2 rows 3[3, 3, 3, 3, 3] (3, 4, 4, 4, 4) [4, 4, 5, 5, 5] more times. Leave sts on needles.

Back shoulders

Worked back and forth on back sts, consuming remaining sleeve stitches with a decrease at the end of each row.

Next row: sl1, k in patt to back left seam st, ssk (working back left seam st together with first st of left sleeve), turn.

Next row (WS): sl1, p across back sts, maintaining charted patt, to back right seam st, p2tog (seam st and 1 sleeve st), turn.

Rep last 2 rows 4[4, 4, 4, 4, 4] (5, 5, 5, 5, 5) [5, 5, 6, 6, 6] more times. 64[64, 68, 70, 70, 72] (76, 78, 78, 80, 84) [86, 86, 88, 92, 92] sts remain for the back.

Prepare steek and join shoulders

Prepare steek by working two lines of slip-stitch crochet (see page 119) working the crochet to join each leg of the centre stitch of the steek with 1 leg of the neighbouring stitch. Cut between the 2 legs of the centre stitch. 3 live steek stitches remain on each side.

Slip 3 sts at right top of steek onto a spare DPN. Slip the 20[21, 21, 22, 22, 23] (25, 25, 25, 26, 27) [28, 27, 28, 29, 29] right front shoulder sts onto a separate DPN. Slip an equal number of back right shoulder sts onto a third DPN. Fold steek to WS to line up live steek sts with live shoulder sts. Fold sweater at shoulder cap so that front and back shoulder sts align with WS facing out. Work a four-needle bind-off to join shoulder seams and live steek sts.

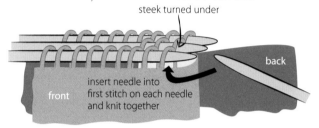

steek turned under

front

back

insert needle into first stitch on each needle and knit together

Join left shoulder and rem steek sts in the same way.

SHAWL COLLAR

Using MC and smaller circular needle, beginning at the bottom right front of placket, pick up and k 2 sts for every 3 rows up right neck, pm, k across 24[24, 26, 26, 26, 26] (26, 28, 28, 28, 30) [30, 32, 32, 34, 34] live back neck sts, pm, pick up and k 2 sts for every 3 rows down left neck, turn. Total number of sts must be an even number, adjust if necessary.

When directed to "turn," remember to prepare the work so that the gap can later be closed. Pam used the wrap and turn technique but other methods, such as the wrapless short row technique (see page 123), can be worked if preferred.

Next row (WS): establish rib pattern as follows, *p2, k2, rep from * to end, ending with k2 or p2.

Next row (RS): work in rib pattern to second marker, at back left neck, remove marker, turn.

Next row (WS): maintaining rib patt, work to marker at back right neck, remove marker, turn.

Next row: maintaining rib patt, work to gap, close gap, work next st in patt, turn.

Rep previous row until all sts have been worked. Work 32[33, 33, 34, 34, 36] (36, 37, 37, 38, 38) [39, 39, 40, 40, 41] more rows in rib patt. Bind off all sts loosely in patt.

FINISHING

Arrange loose bottom edges of collar with the right half on top of the left half. Working from the back, with a tapestry needle and length of MC yarn, tack loose bottom edges of collar to live sts at centre front. Tack down bottom edge of steek to inside of sweater. Graft underarm sts. Weave in all ends and block sweater to measurements.

TUBULAR CAST-ON
(LONG TAIL METHOD)

This cast on is easier to work on a straight needle and is often neater worked with a smaller needle size.

1. Leave a tail approximately four times the desired width of the cast on edge, place yarn over needle held in right hand at this point.

2. Grip both ends in last three fingers of left hand and insert thumb and index finger between strands so that ball end is over index finger.

3. Bring needle to back over and then under index finger strand; bring needle to front over and then under thumb strand, catching it and bringing it up from under index finger strand.

4. Bring needle to front over and then under thumb strand; bring needle to back over and then under index finger strand, catching it and bringing it up from under thumb strand.

Repeat steps 3 and 4 until all stitches have been cast on.

5. Work 2 rows knitting the stitches that present as knits (ktbl on first row) and slipping the stitches that present as purls wyif.

6. For 1x1 rib proceed to pattern. For 2x2 rib rearrange stitches on next row as follows: *k1; insert needle into 2nd stitch on left needle at front from right to left and slip both stitches off, slip dropped st back to left needle, then slip k st from right to left (stitches have been rearranged); k1, p2, rep from * to end.

YARN

Sturdy, minimally processed aran weight yarn. Fisherman 2-ply by Bartlettyarns (100% wool, 210yds / 192m, 3.99oz / 113g) shown in Dark Jade Heather.

1050[1050, 1260, 1260, 1260] (1470, 1470, 1470, 1680)yds / 960[960, 1152, 1152, 1152] (1344, 1344, 1536)m.

NEEDLES AND NOTIONS

US 9 / 5.5mm 32" / 80cm circular needle

US 9 / 5.5mm dpns or needles for preferred method of working small circumferences in the rnd

Scrap yarn

Cable needle

Five ¾" / 19mm buttons

GAUGE

16 sts and 21 rows = 4" / 10cm in st st.

SIZES

Finished chest circumference (buttoned): 35[38, 40, 43, 46] (49, 52, 55, 58)" / 89[97, 101.5, 109, 117] (125, 132, 139.5, 148)cm.

Shown in size 40" with 3½" / 9cm of positive ease.

SPECIAL ABBREVIATIONS

RLI (right lifted increase) — k into the st immediately below the next st

pfb — purl in the front and back of same st

Apple Cider Donut

by Cecily Glowik MacDonald

SCHEMATIC

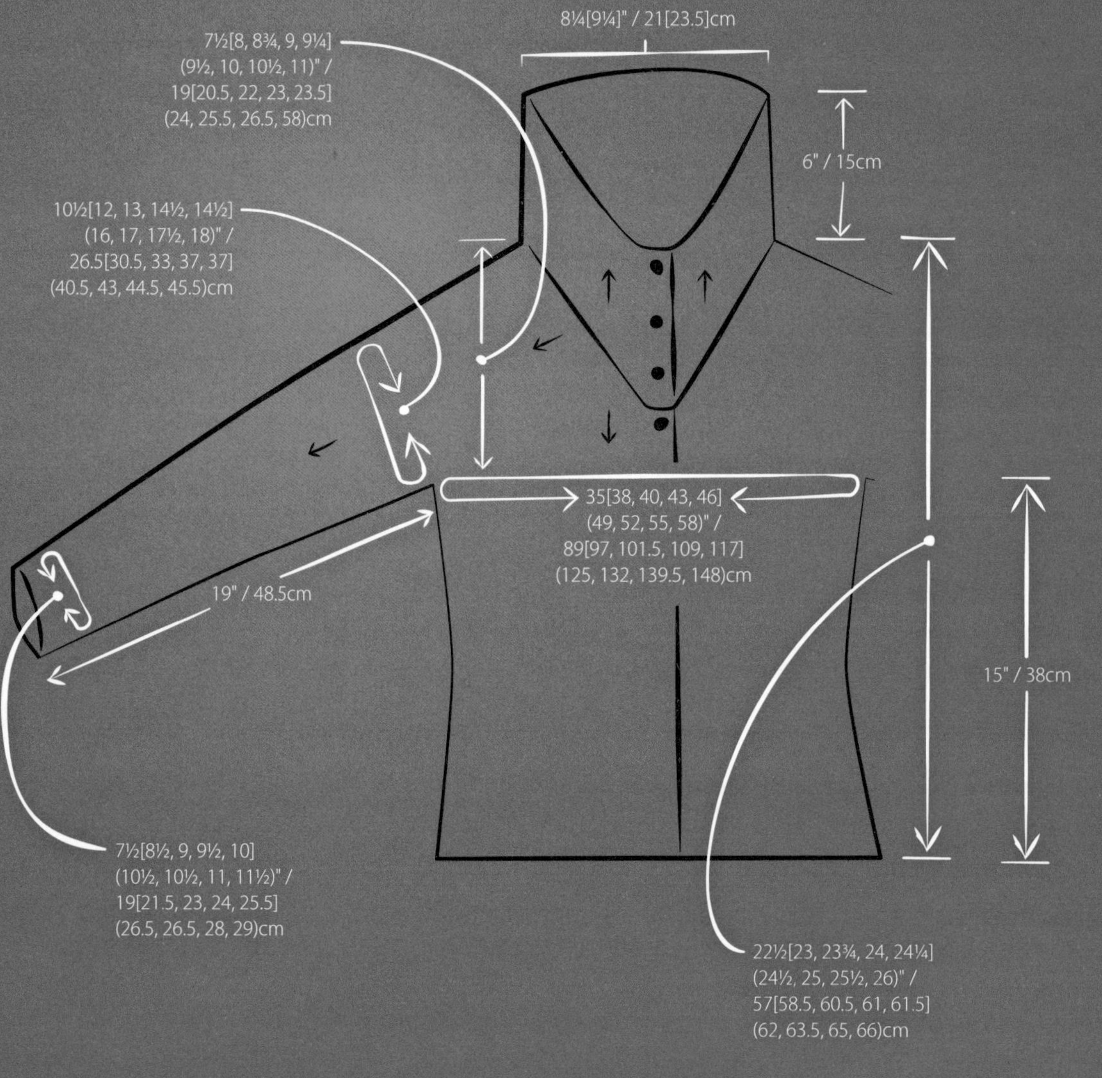

8¼[9¼]" / 21[23.5]cm

6" / 15cm

7½[8, 8¾, 9, 9¼]
(9½, 10, 10½, 11)" /
19[20.5, 22, 23, 23.5]
(24, 25.5, 26.5, 58)cm

10½[12, 13, 14½, 14½]
(16, 17, 17½, 18)" /
26.5[30.5, 33, 37, 37]
(40.5, 43, 44.5, 45.5)cm

35[38, 40, 43, 46]
(49, 52, 55, 58)" /
89[97, 101.5, 109, 117]
(125, 132, 139.5, 148)cm

19" / 48.5cm

15" / 38cm

7½[8½, 9, 9½, 10]
(10½, 10½, 11, 11½)" /
19[21.5, 23, 24, 25.5]
(26.5, 26.5, 28, 29)cm

22½[23, 23¾, 24, 24¼]
(24½, 25, 25½, 26)" /
57[58.5, 60.5, 61, 61.5]
(62, 63.5, 65, 66)cm

Notes

Please read through all Yoke instructions before beginning. Neck shaping, raglan shaping, and buttonhole making take place at the same time.

The neck shaping is worked in two size groups. Follow the first number for sizes 35 – 43" and the second for sizes 46 – 58".

The yoke will be worked in stockinette apart from the ribbing established when the buttonbands are cast on and the increases done on right-side rows.

Directions

YOKE

With circular needles, CO 59 sts.

Row 1 — place raglan markers (WS): p3, pm, p10[8], pm, p33[37], pm, p10[8], pm, p3.

Row 2 — neck inc row: k1, kfb, work to last 3 sts, kfb, k2. 61 sts.

Rep neck inc row every RS row 15[17] more times, working raglan increases at the same time as directed below. When neck incs are complete continue to work raglan incs and cast on for buttonbands as directed below.

Row 3 and all following WS rows: purl all sts until buttonband is cast on.

Row 4 — raglan inc row: inc at neckline as set, *work in patt to 1 st from m, RLI, slm, k1, RLI, rep from * 3 more times, work in patt to last 3 sts, inc as set.

Rep raglan inc row every RS row 7[9, 11, 18, 18] (21, 24, 24, 25) more times, then every 4th row 5[5, 5, 1, 2] (1, 0, 0, 0) more times. 59[63, 67, 73, 79] (83, 87, 87, 89) sts between back markers.

Sizes 52 – 58" only

Next row — body only inc row: *work in patt to 1 st from m, RLI, slm, work in patt to m, slm, k1, RLI, rep from * once more, work in patt to end (1 st inc'd for each front, 2 sts inc'd for back) -[-, -, -, -] (-, 91, 91, 93) sts between back markers.

Repeat body only inc row EVERY row -[-, -, -, -] (-, 0, 2, 4) more times (when working inc's on WS rows work inc as pfb) -[-, -, -, -] (-, 91, 99, 109) sts between markers for back.

All sizes

If necessary, work until yoke measures 7½[8, 8¾, 9, 9¼] (9½, 10, 10½, 11)" / 19[20.5, 22, 23, 23.5] (24, 25.5, 26.5, 28)cm from CO, ending with a WS row.

After all neck and yoke shaping is complete there are 215[231, 247, 271, 287] (303, 323, 331, 347) sts on needles. 42[44, 46, 49, 54] (56, 59, 61, 64) sts for each front, 59[63, 67, 73, 79] (83, 89, 93, 99) sts for back, 36[40, 44, 50, 50] (54, 58, 58, 60) sts for each sleeve.

At the same time

CO for buttonbands after all neck inc rows are complete:

CO 10[12] sts at beg of the next two rows. These new sts will be worked in rib as follows:

RS rows: (k1, p1) 5[6] times, k to 10[12] sts from end, (p1, k1) to end.

WS rows: (p1, k1) 5[6] times, p to 10[12] sts from end, (k1, p1) to end.

When yoke measures ¾" from CO for buttonbands, on next RS row, work buttonhole as follows: work in patt to 4 sts from end, yo, k2tog, p1, k1. Work 15 rows in pattern; then repeat buttonhole row once more. At the same time, follow yoke instructions above.

SEPARATE BODY AND SLEEVES

Next row (RS): maintaining buttonbands, but without further raglan shaping, *work in patt to m, remove m, slip sleeve sts onto scrap yarn, remove m, CO 3[4, 4, 4, 4] (5, 5, 6, 6), pm for side seam, CO 3[4, 4, 4, 4] (5, 5, 6, 6) sts, rep from * once more, work in patt to end. 155[167, 175, 187, 203] (215, 227, 239, 251) sts.

BODY

Work 5 rows in patt, ending with a WS row.

Next row — dec row (RS): *work in patt to 3 sts from m, ssk, k1, slm, k1, k2tog, rep from * once more, work in patt to end. (4 sts dec).

Rep last 6 rows 3[2, 2, 2, 1] (1, 1, 1, 1) more time(s). 139[155, 163, 175, 191] (207, 219, 231, 243) sts.

Sizes 38 – 58" only

Work 3 rows in patt.

Next row: work dec row.

Rep last 4 rows -[0, 0, 0, 1] (1, 1, 1, 1) more time(s). -[151, 159, 171, 187] (199, 211, 223, 235) sts.

Stitch Pattern

COLLAR CABLE PATTERN
multiple of 8 + 3

Rows 1 and 3 (WS): (p1, k1) to last st, p1.

Row 2: *(k1, p1) twice; sl2 sts to cable needle and hold in front, k1, p1; k1, p1 from cable needle; rep from * to last 3 sts; k1, p1, k1.

Row 4: (k1, p1) to last st, k1.

Chart

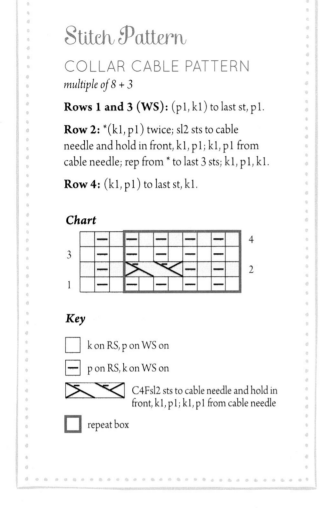

Key

k on RS, p on WS on

p on RS, k on WS on

C4Fsl2 sts to cable needle and hold in front, k1, p1; k1, p1 from cable needle

repeat box

All sizes

Work 7 rows in patt, ending with a WS row.

Next row: *work in patt to 2 sts from m, RLI, k1, slm, k1, RLI, rep from * 1 more time, work in patt to end. (4 sts inc) 143[155, 163, 175, 191] (203, 215, 227, 239) sts.

Work 5 rows in patt.

Rep last 6 rows 4 more times. 159(171, 179, 191, 207, 219, 231, 243, 255) sts.

Work even until body measures 14" / 35.5cm ending with a WS row.

Rib trim

Next row (RS): (k1, p1) to 1 st from end, k1.

Next row: (p1, k1) to 1 st from end, p1.

Work in rib as est for 1" / 2.5cm, ending with a WS row.

Next row (RS): bind off in patt, being careful not to bind off too tightly.

SLEEVES

Transfer held sts for sleeves onto dpns (or preferred needles for working small circumferences in the rnd).

With RS facing, join yarn and pick up and knit 6[8, 8, 8, 8] (10, 10, 12, 12) sts from cast-on sts at underarm. 42[48, 52, 58, 58] (64, 68, 70, 72) sts.

K 1 rnd, then k3[4, 4, 4, 4] (5, 5, 6, 6) sts to the centre of the picked up stitches, and pm to mark end of rnd.

K 8 rnds.

***Next rnd — dec rnd:** k1, k2tog, work to last 3 sts, ssk, k1. 40[46, 50, 56, 56] (62, 66, 68, 70) sts rem.

K 17[17, 13, 9, 13] (9, 7, 7, 7) rnds.

Rep from * 2[0, 2, 4, 0] (0, 4, 4, 4) more time(s). 34[42, 44, 46, 54] (60, 56, 58, 60) sts rem.

****Rep dec rnd.

K 13[12, 9, 7, 9] (7, 5, 5, 5) rnds.

Rep from ** 1[4, 3, 3, 6] (8, 6, 6, 6) more time(s).

Work dec rnd once more.

Work even until sleeve measures 18" / 46cm from underarm.

Rib cuff

Next rnd: (k1, p1) to end.

Work in rib as est for 1" / 2.5cm.

Bind off in patt. Rep for second sleeve.

FINISHING

Block to measurements.

COLLAR

The collar is worked in two size groups. Follow the first number for size 35 – 43, and the second for sizes 46 – 58.

With RS facing, beg at CO sts for buttonhole band on right front, pick up and knit 32[36] sts from right front to initial CO, pick up and knit 59 sts from initial CO, pick up and knit 32[36] sts down left front including CO sts for band. 123[131] sts.

Work 7 rows in collar cable pattern beg and ending with a WS row.

Next row — buttonhole row (RS): *k1, p1, k2tog, yo, work in patt to end.

Work in patt for 11 rows.

Repeat last 12 rows once more.

Work buttonhole row once more.

Work 6 rows in patt, ending with a RS row.

Bind off loosely in pattern.

FINISHING

Block collar. Sew buttons on to match buttonholes.

· · · · · · ● · · · · · ·

YARN

Worsted weight yarn with good elasticity; wool or wool blends are ideal. Shown in The Verdant Gryphon Mondegreen (60% Blue-faced Leicester, 20% silk, 20% baby camel, 200yds / 183m, 4oz / 113g) in She Was a Fax Machine

Contrast yarn: lace weight yarn such as wool or silk. Shown in The Verdant Gryphon Mithril (100% Merino wool, 750yds / 686m, 4oz / 113g) in Poynter's Andromeda

Worsted Weight 1085[1200, 1330, 1430, 1560] (1720, 1870, 2010)yds / 990[1095, 1220, 1310, 1425) [1575, 1710, 1840]m.

Lace Weight 1020[1130, 1250, 1340, 1460] (1610, 1750, 1885)yds / 935(1035, 1145, 1225, 1335) [1475, 1605, 1725]m.

NEEDLES AND NOTIONS

US 8 / 5mm 24" / 60cm circular needle and dpns or circulars for your preferred method of knitting small circumferences in the rnd

Stitch markers, including removable markers

Four ⅝" / 13cm buttons

GAUGE

18 sts and 22 rnds = 4" / 10cm in st st in the rnd with both yarns held together.

21 sts and 28 rnds = 4" / 10cm in Texture Stitch in the rnd with both yarns held together.

SIZES

Finished chest circumference: 32¾[35¾, 38¾, 41¼, 44¼] (47¼, 50¼, 53¼)" / 83[91, 98.5, 103.5, 113.5] (121.5, 129, 136.5)cm.

Shown in size 32¾" with 1¼" / 3cm of negative ease.

Mulberry Street

by Melissa Wehrle

SCHEMATIC

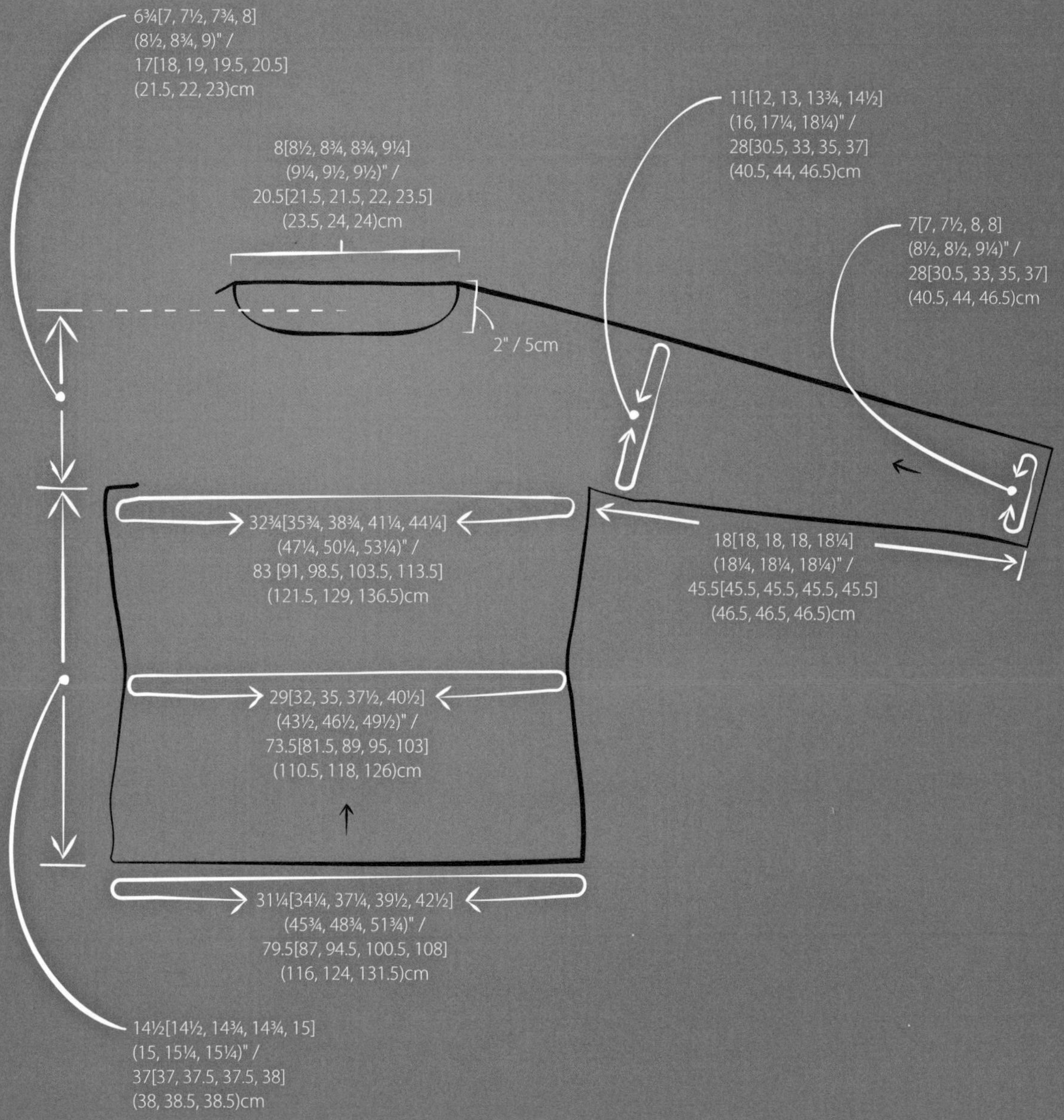

6¾[7, 7½, 7¾, 8]
(8½, 8¾, 9)" /
17[18, 19, 19.5, 20.5]
(21.5, 22, 23)cm

8[8½, 8¾, 8¾, 9¼]
(9¼, 9½, 9½)" /
20.5[21.5, 21.5, 22, 23.5]
(23.5, 24, 24)cm

11[12, 13, 13¾, 14½]
(16, 17¼, 18¼)" /
28[30.5, 33, 35, 37]
(40.5, 44, 46.5)cm

7[7, 7½, 8, 8]
(8½, 8½, 9¼)" /
28[30.5, 33, 35, 37]
(40.5, 44, 46.5)cm

2" / 5cm

32¾[35¾, 38¾, 41¼, 44¼]
(47¼, 50¼, 53¼)" /
83 [91, 98.5, 103.5, 113.5]
(121.5, 129, 136.5)cm

18[18, 18, 18, 18¼]
(18¼, 18¼, 18¼)" /
45.5[45.5, 45.5, 45.5, 45.5]
(46.5, 46.5, 46.5)cm

29[32, 35, 37½, 40½]
(43½, 46½, 49½)" /
73.5[81.5, 89, 95, 103]
(110.5, 118, 126)cm

31¼[34¼, 37¼, 39½, 42½]
(45¾, 48¾, 51¾)" /
79.5[87, 94.5, 100.5, 108]
(116, 124, 131.5)cm

14½[14½, 14¾, 14¾, 15]
(15, 15¼, 15¼)" /
37[37, 37.5, 37.5, 38]
(38, 38.5, 38.5)cm

Stitch Patterns

TEXTURE STITCH, IN THE RND
multiple of 2

Rnd 1: k.

Rnd 2: (k1, p1) to end.

TEXTURE STITCH, IN ROWS
multiple of 2 +1

Row 1 (RS): k.

Row 2: (p1, k1) last st, p1.

Directions

BODY

With MC and CC yarns held together, CO 164[180, 196, 208, 224] (240, 256, 272) sts.

Join rnd and pm to mark EOR, work 1x1 rib over 82[90, 98, 104, 112] (120, 128, 136) sts pm to indicate side seam, continue in rib to EOR.

Work in 1x1 rib for 1¼"/ 3cm.

Change to texture stitch and work even in patt until body measures 3" / 7.5cm from CO edge.

**Next rnd — dec rnd: *k1, k2tog, work in patt to 2 sts from m, ssk, slm, rep from * once more.

Work 13[13, 13, 13, 13] (13, 15, 15) rnds in patt.

Rep from ** 1[1, 0, 0, 0] (0, 1, 1) more time. 156[172, 192, 204, 220] (236, 248, 264) sts.

Sizes 38¾ – 47" only

Rep dec rnd. Work -[-, 15, 15, 15] (15, -, -) rnds in patt. -[-, 188, 200, 216] (232, -, -) sts.

All sizes

Work dec rnd once more.
152[168, 184, 196, 212] (228, 244, 260) sts.

Work even in patt until body measures 8¼[8¼, 8 ½, 8½, 8½] (8½, 8¾, 8¾)" / 21[21, 21.5, 21.5, 21.5] (21.5, 22, 22)cm from CO edge.

**Next rnd — inc rnd: *k1, m1, work in patt to m, m1, slm, rep from * once more.

Work 5[5, 5, 5, 7] (7, 7, 7) rnds in patt.

Rep from ** 1[1, 1, 1, 4] (4, 4, 4) more time(s). 160[176, 192, 204, 232] (248, 264, 280) sts.

Sizes 32¾ – 41¼" only

***Rep inc rnd. Work in patt for 7[7, 7, 7, -] (-, -, -) rnds

Rep from *** 2[2, 2, 2, -] (-, -, -) more time(s).

172[188, 204, 216, -] (-, -, -) sts.

All sizes

Body will measure approx 13½[13½, 13¾, 13¾, 14¼] (14¼, 14½, 14½)" / 34[34, 35, 35, 36] (36, 37, 37)cm from CO edge.

Next rnd: work in patt to m, slm, k2[2, 2, 1, 1] (1, 1, 1), [k3tog, k7[8, 9, 10, 11] (12, 13, 14)] 8 times, k3tog, k1[1, 1, 0, 0] (0, 0, 0).

86[94, 102, 108, 116] (124, 132, 140) front sts, 68[76, 84, 90, 98] (106, 114, 122) back sts.

Next rnd: work in patt to m, slm, work in 1x1 rib to end of rnd. Work even in patt as set (texture stitch in front, 1x1 rib in back) for 1" / 2cm ending with a rnd 1 in patt for front.

Divide for armholes: work in patt to 4[5, 6, 7, 8] (8, 9, 11) sts before m, BO 76[86, 96, 104, 114] (122, 132, 144) sts, removing markers as you come to them. 78[84, 90, 94, 100] (108, 114, 118) sts rem for front. Set aside body as you work on the sleeves.

SLEEVES — MAKE TWO

With MC and CC yarns held together, CO 36[36, 40, 42, 42] (44, 44, 48) sts. Join rnd and pm to mark EOR.

Work in 1x1 rib for 1¼" / 3cm.

Next rnd: change to texture stitch.

*Next rnd: k1, m1, work in patt to 1 st before EOR, m1.

Work 9[7, 7, 5, 5] (3, 3, 3) rnds in patt.

Rep from * 6[11, 11, 2, 9] (2, 11, 14) more times.

*Next rnd: k1, m1, work in patt to 1 st before EOR, m1.

Work 11[9, 9, 7, 7] (5, 5, 5) rnds in patt.

Rep from * 2[0, 0, 10, 5] (15, 9, 7) more times.

Rep inc rnd once more. 58[64, 68, 72, 76] (84, 90, 96) sts.

Work even until sleeve measures 18[18, 18, 18, 18¼] (18¼, 18¼, 18¼, 18¼)" / 45.5[45.5, 45.5, 45.5, 46.5] (46.5, 46.5, 46.5)cm from CO, ending with rnd 1 of texture stitch.

Next rnd: work in patt to 4[5, 6, 7, 8] (8, 9, 10] sts before EOR, BO 8[10, 12, 14, 16] (16, 18, 22) sts, removing m when you come to it. 50[54, 56, 58, 60] (68, 72, 74) sts.

Place all sts on scrap yarn and set aside.

UPPER BODY

The body will now be worked back and forth in rows.

When directed to work in pattern in following directions work all WS rows in texture stitch and knit all RS rows.

With RS facing, k across first sleeve, k across front sts, k across second sleeve. Backwards loop CO 40[42, 46, 48, 50] (54, 58, 60) sts for right back. 218[234, 248, 258, 270] (298, 316, 326) sts.

Next row (WS): work in texture stitch to end, backwards loop CO 39[41, 45, 47, 49] (53, 57, 59) sts for left back. 257[275, 293, 305, 319] (351, 373, 385) sts.

Work 2 rows in patt.

Note: raglan yoke shaping and short-row shaping for back keyhole are worked at the same time beg on the next row. Short-rows to shape the neckline are started before armhole shaping is complete. Please read ahead in pattern.

When directed to "turn," remember to prepare the work so that the gap can later be closed. Melissa used the wrap and turn method, but other methods, such as the wrapless turn (see p. 123), can be worked if preferred.

Raglan shaping and back keyhole short-rows:

Next row (RS): k34[36, 40, 42, 44] (48, 52, 54) sts, k3tog, pm, k5, pm, sssk, k39[43, 45, 47, 49] (57, 61, 63) sts, k3tog, pm, k5, pm, sssk, k67[73, 79, 83, 89] (97, 103, 107) sts, k3tog, pm, k5, pm, sssk, k39[43, 45, 47, 49] (57, 61, 63) sts, k3tog, pm, k5, pm, sssk, k to last 4[5, 5, 5, 6] (6, 7, 7) sts, turn. 241[259, 277, 289, 303] (335, 357, 369) sts.

Next row (WS): work in patt to 4[5, 5, 5, 6] (6, 7, 7) sts from end, turn.

Next 4[4, 4, 2, 2] (2, 2, 2) rows: work even in patt to 4[5, 5, 5, 6] (6, 7, 7) sts from previous gap, turn.

**Next row — dec row (RS): *k to 3 sts before m, k3tog, slm, k5, slm, sssk; rep from * 3 more times, k to 4[5, 5, 5, 6] (6, 7, 7) sts from previous gap, turn. 225[243, 261, 273, 287] (319, 341, 353) sts.

Next 5[3, 3, 3, 3] (3, 3, 3) rows: work in patt to 4[5, 5, 5, 6] (6, 7, 7) sts from previous gap, turn.

Rep from ** 0[1, 1, 1, 1] (1, 1, 1] more time(s).

Work dec row once more. 209[211, 229, 241, 255] (287, 309, 321)

Next 3[1, 1, 3, 3] (3, 3, 3) row(s): work in patt to 4[5, 5, 5, 6, 6, 7, 7] sts from previous gap, turn.

Sizes 32¾ – 38¾"

Next row: k across all sts, closing gaps as you come to them.

Sizes 41½ – 51¾"

Next row: *k to 3 sts before m, k3tog, slm, k5, slm, sssk; rep from * 3 more times, k across rem sts, closing gaps as you come to them. -[-, -, 225, 239] (271, 293, 305) sts.

All sizes

Next row: work in patt across all sts, closing gaps as you come to them.

Work 0[0, 0, 2, 2] (2, 2, 2) rows even in patt.

Next row (RS): *k to 3 sts before m, k3tog, slm, k5, slm, sssk; rep from * 3 more times.

Work 3 rows even in patt.

Rep last 4 rows 5[5, 6, 6, 7] (6, 5, 5) more times. 113[115, 117, 113, 111] (159, 197, 209) sts.

Sizes 47¼ – 51¾"

Next row (RS): *k to 3 sts before m, k3tog, slm, k5, slm, sssk; rep from * 3 more times.

Work 1 row even in patt.

Rep last 2 rows -[-, -, -, -] (2, 4, 5) more times. -[-, -, -, -] (111, 117, 113) sts.

All sizes

Work even until body measures 6¾[7, 7½, 7¾, 8] (8½, 8¾, 9)" / 17[18, 19, 19.5, 20.5] (21.5, 22, 23) cm from underarm when measured straight (not along raglan line).

At the same time

When back yoke measures 3[3¼, 3¾, 4, 4¼] (4¾, 5, 5¼)" / 7.5[8.5, 9.5, 10, 11] (12, 12.5, 13.5)cm from CO, beg short-row shaping for neck on the next RS row: pm at either side of the 15[15, 17, 17] (17, 19, 19) front centre neck sts.

Left neck

Next row (RS): k to 7[8, 8, 7, 8] (8, 8, 7) sts from m, turn.

Next row: work in patt to end.

Next row: k to 7[8, 8, 7, 8] (8, 8, 7) sts from gap, turn.

Next row: work in patt to end.

Rep last 2 rows 4 more times.

Next row (RS): k across all sts, closing gaps as you come to them, k to end.

Right neck

Next row (WS): work in patt to 7[8, 8, 7, 8] (8, 8, 7) sts from m, turn.

Next row: k to end.

Next row: work in patt to 7[8, 8, 7, 8] (8, 8, 7) sts from gap, turn.

Next row: k to end.

Rep last 2 rows 4 more times.

Next row (WS): work in patt across all sts, closing gaps as you come to them, work in patt to end.

Change to 1x1 rib and work 6 rows even. Bind off loosely.

FINISHING

Sew bound off underarm sts together, then continuing from the armhole seam, sew approximately 2" / 5cm of the bound off back edge and the cast on edge of the upper back together on each side. Try on sweater and pin centre back pieces together, overlapping the right back over the left back. Sew centre back edges together. Sew on 4 buttons at centre back placket, spacing evenly. Weave in all ends.

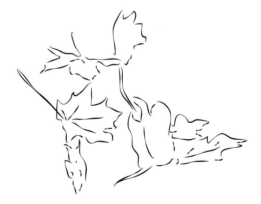

YARN

Aran weight yarn with good stitch definition. Shown in Jill Draper Makes Stuff Empire (100% Rambouillet wool, 1280yds / 1170m, 27oz / 770g) in Leaf.

790[860, 910, 960, 1030, 1100] (1150, 1180, 1280, 1360, 1450) [1490, 1540, 1630, 1650, 1790]yds / 720[790, 840, 880, 940, 1010] (1010, 1050, 1080, 1170, 1240) [1320, 1360, 1410, 1490, 1640]m.

NEEDLES AND NOTIONS

US 9 / 5mm 16" / 40cm, 24" / 60cm, and 32" / 80cm circular needles

US 9 / 5mm dpns or circulars for your preferred method of working small circumferences in the rnd

US 8 / 4mm 24" / 60cm and 32" / 80cm circular needles

US 8 / 4mm dpns or circulars for your preferred method of working small circumferences in the rnd

12 stitch markers, 4 of colour A, and 8 of colour B

Scrap yarn

GAUGE

14 sts and 21 rnds = 4" / 10cm on larger needle in st st in the rnd.

Artichoke Stitch Side Panel = 30 sts = 7" / 18 cm.

SIZES

Finished chest circumference: 27½[30, 32½, 34, 36, 37] (40, 41½, 44, 45½, 47½) [49½, 52½, 54, 56, 57½]" / 70[76, 82.5, 86.5, 91.5, 96.5] (101.5, 105.5, 112, 115.5, 120.5) [125.5, 133.5, 137, 142, 146]cm.

Shown in size 30" with 1" / 2.5cm negative ease.

Artichoke French

by Laura Nelkin

SCHEMATIC

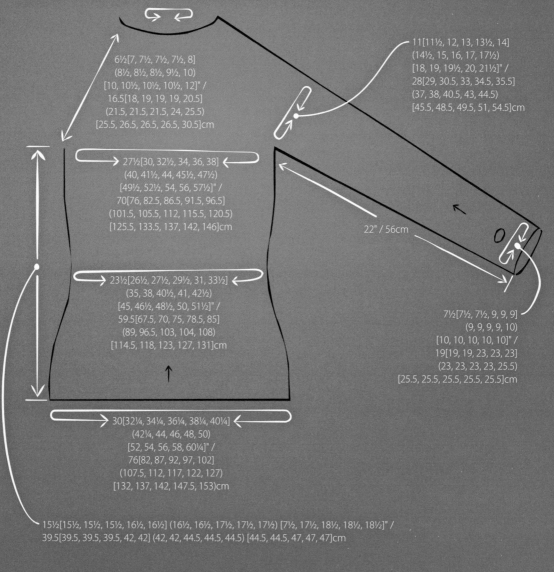

20½[23, 23, 23, 23, 25½] (25½, 25½, 25½, 25½, 28½) [28½, 28½, 28½, 28½, 28½]" /
52[58.5, 58.5, 58.5, 58.5, 65] (65, 65, 65, 65, 72.5) [72.5, 72.5, 72.5, 72.5, 72.5]cm

6½[7, 7½, 7½, 7½, 8]
(8½, 8½, 8½, 9½, 10)
[10, 10½, 10½, 10½, 12]" /
16.5[18, 19, 19, 19, 20.5]
(21.5, 21.5, 21.5, 24, 25.5)
[25.5, 26.5, 26.5, 26.5, 30.5]cm

11[11½, 12, 13, 13½, 14]
(14½, 15, 16, 17, 17½)
[18, 19, 19½, 20, 21½]" /
28[29, 30.5, 33, 34.5, 35.5]
(37, 38, 40.5, 43, 44.5)
[45.5, 48.5, 49.5, 51, 54.5]cm

27½[30, 32½, 34, 36, 38]
(40, 41½, 44, 45½, 47½)
[49½, 52½, 54, 56, 57½]" /
70[76, 82.5, 86.5, 91.5, 96.5]
(101.5, 105.5, 112, 115.5, 120.5)
[125.5, 133.5, 137, 142, 146]cm

22" / 56cm

23½[26½, 27½, 29½, 31, 33½]
(35, 38, 40½, 41, 42½)
[45, 46½, 48½, 50, 51½]" /
59.5[67.5, 70, 75, 78.5, 85]
(89, 96.5, 103, 104, 108)
[114.5, 118, 123, 127, 131]cm

7½[7½, 7½, 9, 9, 9]
(9, 9, 9, 9, 10)
[10, 10, 10, 10, 10]" /
19[19, 19, 23, 23, 23]
(23, 23, 23, 23, 25.5)
[25.5, 25.5, 25.5, 25.5, 25.5]cm

30[32¼, 34¼, 36¼, 38¼, 40¼]
(42¼, 44, 46, 48, 50)
[52, 54, 56, 58, 60¼]" /
76[82, 87, 92, 97, 102]
(107.5, 112, 117, 122, 127)
[132, 137, 142, 147.5, 153]cm

15½[15½, 15½, 15½, 16½, 16½] (16½, 16½, 17½, 17½, 17½) [7½, 17½, 18½, 18½, 18½]" /
39.5[39.5, 39.5, 39.5, 42, 42] (42, 42, 44.5, 44.5, 44.5) [44.5, 44.5, 47, 47, 47]cm

Stitch Pattern

ARTICHOKE STITCH
worked over a multiple of 9 + 3 sts

Rnd 1: (p3, k1 wrapping twice, k4, k1 wrapping twice), p3.

Rnd 2: (p3, sl1 dropping extra wrap, k4, sl1 dropping extra wrap), p3.

Rnd 3: (p3, sl1, k4, sl1), p3.

Rnd 4: (p3, drop st, hold in front, k2, knit dropped stitch, sl2 purlwise onto right needle, drop next st, sl2 back to left needle, knit dropped st, k2), p3.

Note

WORKING THE THUMBHOLE

Depending on the yarn you use you might decide that your thumbhole doesn't have enough "structure". If this is the case, then work a single crochet around it to tighten it up.

Directions

BODY

With smaller circular needle, CO 114[124, 132, 138, 144, 152] (158, 164, 172, 178, 184) [192, 198, 208, 214, 224] sts. Join rnd and pm to mark EOR.

Ribbing

Ribbing Rnd 1: *p30, pmB, k2[2, 4, 3, 2, 4] (3, 2, 4, 3, 2) [4, 3, 3, 2, 2], (p3, k2) 5[6, 6, 7, 8, 8] (9, 10, 10, 11, 12) [12, 13, 14, 15, 16] times, k0[0, 2, 1, 0, 2] (1, 0, 2, 1, 0) [2, 1, 1, 0, 0], pmB, rep from * once.

Next rnd: *work rnd 1 of Artichoke Stitch over 30 sts, slm, work in patt to m, slm, rep from * once.

Work 7 rnds in patt as established in previous rnd.

Switch to larger needle.

Next rnd: *work next rnd of Artichoke Stitch as established, slm, knit to m, slm, rep from * once.

Work 4[4, 3, 3, 3, 3] (3, 4, 4, 3, 3) [3, 3, 3, 3, 2] rnds in patt as established in previous rnd.

Waist decreases

**Next rnd — dec rnd: *work next rnd of Artichoke Stitch as established, slm, ssk, k to 2 sts before m, k2tog, slm, rep from * once.

Work even in patt for 5[5, 4, 4, 4, 4] (4, 5, 5, 4, 4) [4, 4, 4, 4, 3] rnds. (4 sts dec).

Rep from ** 3[3, 4, 4, 4, 4] (4, 3, 3, 4, 4) [4, 4, 5, 5, 6] more times.

Work dec rnd once more. 94[104, 108, 114, 120, 128] (134, 144, 152, 154, 160) [168, 174, 180, 186, 192] sts.

Work 9[9, 9, 9, 9, 9] (9, 9, 9, 9, 9) [9, 9, 9, 4, 7] rnds even in patt.

Waist increases

**Next rnd — inc rnd: *work next rnd of Artichoke Stitch as established, slm, k1, m1R, k to 1 st before m, m1L, k1, slm, rep from * once.

Work even in patt for 9[9, 7, 7, 8, 8] (8, 10, 11, 9, 9) [9, 7, 8, 8, 8] rnds. (4 sts inc).

Rep from ** 2 more times.

Work inc rnd once more. 110[120, 124, 130, 136, 144] (150, 160, 168, 170, 176) [184, 190, 196, 202, 208] sts.

Continue working even in patt until body measures 15½[15½, 15½, 15½, 16½, 16½] (16½, 16½, 17½, 17½, 17½) [17½, 17½, 18½, 18½, 18½]" / 39[39, 39, 39, 41, 41] (41, 41, 44, 44, 44) [44, 44, 46, 46, 46] cm from CO edge or until desired length to underarm, ending with rnd 2 of Artichoke Stitch.

Sizes 30, 32½, 40, 49½, 54 and 57½"
Work 1 rnd even.

Sizes 27½, 34, 36, 41½, 44, 45½, and 56"
Work 1 rnd, dec 1[-, -, 1, 2, -] (-, 3, 3, 2, -) [-, -, -, 1, -] sts on both front and back, spacing decreases evenly in st st sections between markers.

Sizes 37, 47½, and 52½"
Work 1 rnd, inc -[-, -, -, -, 1] (-, -, -, -, 2) [-, 1, -, -, -] sts on both front and back, spacing increases evenly in st st sections between markers. 108[120, 124, 128, 132, 146] (150, 154, 162, 166, 180) [184, 192, 196, 200, 208] sts.

Setting up for joining body and sleeves

Next rnd: *work 18 sts in Artichoke Stitch, place last 6 sts worked on scrap yarn, work 12 sts in Artichoke Stitch, slm, k to m, slm, rep from * once more.

SLEEVES

Handwarmer section of sleeves is worked in 3 size groups. Follow the first number for size 27½ – 32½, the second for sizes 34 – 45½ and the third for sizes 47½ – 57½.

With smaller needles for your preferred method of working small circumferences in the rnd, CO 29[34, 39] sts. Join rnd and pm to mark EOR.

Ribbing

Set Up rnd: k0[2,0] (p3, k2) 2[2, 3] times, pmA, p12, pmA, k2, (p3, k2) 1[1, 2] time(s), p0[3, 0].

Next rnd: work in patt to m, slm, work rnd 1 of Artichoke Stitch, slm, work in patt to end.

Work 8 more rnds in patt as established in previous rnd, ending with rnd 1 of Artichoke Stitch.

Thumbhole rnds right sleeve ONLY

Work in patt to 5 sts before m, bring yarn to front, sl1, bring yarn to back, **drop yarn**, *sl1, then pass 1st slipped st over 2nd slipped st (this binds off 1 st); rep from * 4 more times removing marker when you come to it, sl last st back to left needle, **turn work**.

With working yarn and cable cast-on, CO 7 sts; **turn work**. Sl last CO st onto left needle pmA, p2tog (joining last CO st to adjacent st), p2, sl1, k4, sl1, p3, slm, work in patt to end. 30[35, 40] sts.

Thumbhole rnds left sleeve ONLY

Work in patt to m, slm, work rnd 2 of Artichoke Stitch to m, slm, bring yarn to front, slip 1 stitch, bring yarn to back, **drop yarn**, *sl1, then pass 1st slipped st over 2nd slipped st (this binds off 1 st); rep from * 4 more times, sl last st back to left needle, **turn work**. With working yarn and cable cast-on, CO 7 sts; **turn work**. Sl last CO st onto left needle, k2tog (joining last CO st to adjacent st), k1, work in patt to end. 30[35, 40] sts.

Both sleeves

Switch to larger needles.

Next rnd: k to m, work rnd 3 of Artichoke Stitch, knit to end. Continue in patt as est in previous rnd until sleeve measures 6" / 15cm from CO edge.

*Work 11[9, 8, 10, 8, 6] (6, 6, 5, 5, 5) [4, 4, 3, 3, 3] rnds in patt.

Next rnd: k1, m1L, work in patt to 1 st from end, m1R, k1.

Rep from * 5[6, 7, 5, 6, 7] (8, 9, 11, 12, 11) [12, 14, 15, 16, 18] more times. 42[44, 46, 47, 49, 51] (53, 55, 59, 61, 64) [66, 70, 72, 74, 78] sts.

Sizes 35 – 46½ only

Work -[-, -, 10, 8, 6] (6, 6, 5, 5, -) [-, -, -, -, -] rnds in patt.

Next rnd: k1, m1L, work in patt to end. -[-, -, 48, 50, 52] (54, 56, 60, 62, -) [-, -, -, -, -] sts.

All sizes

Work in patt until sleeve measures approx. 22" / 56cm from CO edge, or until desired length to underarm, ending with rnd 4 of Artichoke Stitch, and, on final rnd, stop 3 sts from end.

Place next 6 sts on scrap yarn, removing EOR m. Cut yarn leaving a 8" / 20 cm tail. Slip sleeve sts onto scrap yarn.

Work second sleeve, working thumbhole for left hand.

Hint: Keep track of which is your right and left sleeve, this will be important when you connect them for the yoke!

JOINING THE BODY AND SLEEVES FOR THE YOKE

Note: Artichoke Stitch panel will continue up the sleeves to the neck as set. While working the raglan shaping, the 8 B markers in the following round mark the decrease points. When directed to work in patt to marker, work the sleeve sts in patt as established, slipping A markers on either side of Artichoke Stitch and work to the next raglan marker (mB).

Switch to 16" / 40cm circular when necessary.

Next rnd: *work rnd 1 of Artichoke Stitch, pmB, return left sleeve sts to needles and work across all live sts in patt as set, pmB, work rnd 1 of Artichoke Stitch, slmB, k to m, slmB, rep from * once more. 168[184, 192, 200, 208, 226] (234, 242, 258, 266, 284) [292, 308, 316, 324, 340] sts.

Work 1 rnd in patt as established in previous rnd.

Beg raglan decreases as follows:

Next rnd — dec rnd: *work in patt to mB, slmB, k2tog, work sleeve in patt to 2 sts before mB, ssk, slmB, work in patt to mB, slmB, ssk, knit to 2 sts before mB, k2tog, slmB, rep from * once more. (8 sts dec).

Work 1 rnd in patt.

Rep last 2 rnds 0[1, 1, 2, 3, 4] (4, 5, 6, 6, 6) [6, 8, 8, 9, 9] more time(s). 160[168, 176, 176, 176, 186] (194, 194, 202, 210, 228) [236, 236, 244, 244, 260] sts.

Rep dec rnd.

Work 3 rnds in patt.

Rep last 4 rnds 5[6, 6, 5, 4, 4] (4, 3, 2, 4, 4) [3, 2, 1, 0, 2] more time(s). 104[112, 120, 128, 136, 146] (154, 162, 178, 170, 188) [204, 212, 228, 236, 236] sts.

Rep dec rnd.

Work 1 rnd in patt.

Rep last 2 rnds 3[2, 3, 4, 5, 5] (6, 7, 9, 8, 9) [11, 12, 14, 15, 15] more time(s). 88[88, 88, 88, 88, 98] (98, 98, 98, 98, 108) [108, 108, 108, 108, 108] sts.

Next rnd: *work in patt to 3 sts before mB, p2, p2tog (removing m), work sleeve in patt to 2 sts from mB, p2togtbl, slmB, work next rnd of Artichoke Stitch, ssk, k to 2 sts from mB, k2tog, slmB, rep from * once more. 80[80, 80, 80, 80, 90] (90, 90, 90, 90, 100) [100, 100, 100, 100, 100] sts.

If necessary, work in patt until Rnd 4 of Artichoke Stitch has been worked.

Neckline band

The neckband is worked perpendicular to the neckline and attached to the live stitches around the neck as you go.

Cut yarn, leaving a 6" / 15cm tail.

With RS facing and scrap yarn, provisionally CO 8 sts onto left needle.

***Row 1:** sl1 wyib, p1, k1 wrapping yarn twice, k2, k1 wrapping yarn twice, p1, sl1, k1 (from neckline sts), psso. Turn work.

Row 2: sl1 wyif, k1, sl1 wyif dropping extra wrap, p2, sl1 wyif dropping extra wrap, k1, p1. Turn work.

Row 3: sl1 wyib, p1, sl1 wyib, k2, sl1 wyib, p1, sl1, k1 (from neckline sts), psso. Turn work.

Row 4: sl1 wyif, k1, drop next st and hold in back, p1, p dropped st, sl1 purlwise onto right needle, drop next st, sl st back to left needle, purl dropped st, p1, k1, p1. Turn work.

Row 5: sl1 wyib, p1, k1 wrapping yarn twice, k2, k1 wrapping yarn twice, p1, sl1, k1 (from neckline sts), psso. Turn work.

Row 6: sl1 wyif, k1, sl1 wyif dropping extra wrap, p2, sl1 wyif dropping extra wrap, k1, p1. Turn work.

Row 7: sl1 wyib, p1, sl1 wyib, k2, sl1 wyib, p1, sl1, k2tog (from neckline sts), psso. Turn work.

Row 8: sl1 wyif, k1, drop st, hold in back, p1, purl dropped stitch, sl1 purlwise onto right needle, drop next st, sl st back to left needle, purl dropped st, p1, k1, p1. Turn work.

Rep from * 15[15, 15, 15, 15, 17] (17, 17, 17, 17, 19) [19, 19, 19, 19, 19] more times, until all necklines stitches are worked.

Grafting Collar in Pattern

Cut yarn leaving a 20" / 50cm tail and Kitchener stitch ends of neckline band together as follows:

Set up
Go into the first stitch on the front needle (FN) as if to purl and leave on the needle,

Go into the first stitch on the back needle (BN) as if to knit and leave on the needle, **then:**

Step 1
Go into the first stitch on the FN as if to knit and slip off the needle,

go into the next stitch on the FN as if to purl and leave on the needle,

go into the first stitch on the BN as if to purl and slip off the needle,

go into the next stitch on the BN as if to knit and leave on the needle.

Step 2
Go into the first stitch on the FN as if to purl and slip off the needle,

go into the next stitch on the FN as if to knit and leave on the needle,

go into the first stitch on the BN as if to knit and slip off the needle,

go into the next stitch on the BN as if to purl and leave on the needle.

Rep step 1 four times more.

Rep step 2 once more.

Finish
Go into the first stitch on the FN as if to knit and slip off the needle, go into the first stitch on the BN as if to purl and slip off the needle. Pull tail through last stitch and fasten off.

FINISHING

Kitchener stitch underarm sts, weave in all ends and block to measurements.

· · · · · · · ● · · · · · · ·

Spring Brook

by Connie Chang Chinchio

YARN

Fingering weight yarn with good drape and clear stitch definition. Two ply yarns, such as the one shown, will show the yarn overs particularly clearly.

Bijou Basin Tibetan Dream Sock (85% yak, 15% nylon, 440yds / 402m, 3.99oz / 113g) shown in #07 Sage.

800[860, 940, 1020] (1100, 1200, 1270)yds / 720[790, 890, 940] (1020, 1090, 1170)m.

NEEDLES AND NOTIONS

US 4 / 3.5 mm 24" / 60cm or longer circular needle

US 3 / 3.25 mm 24" / 60cm or longer circular needle

Stitch markers

Scrap yarn

GAUGE

22 sts and 30 rows = 4" / 10 cm in st st on larger needles, blocked.

SIZES

Finished back chest (below underarm): 17¼[19, 21, 22¾] (24½, 26¼, 28¼)" / 44[48.5, 53, 57.5] (62.5, 67, 71.5)cm.

Shown in smallest size with approx. 1"/2.5cm of positive ease across the back. Choose a size 1-2"/2.5-5cm larger than half of your chest measurement when measured at underarm level.

SCHEMATIC

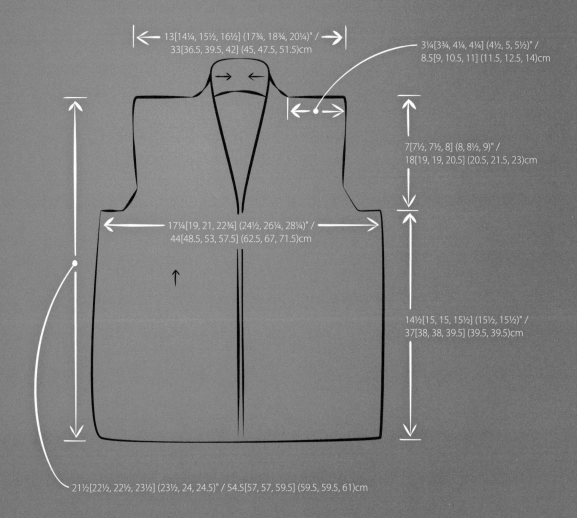

13[14¼, 15½, 16½] (17¾, 18¾, 20¼)" / 33[36.5, 39.5, 42] (45, 47.5, 51.5)cm

3¼[3¾, 4¼, 4¼] (4½, 5, 5½)" / 8.5[9, 10.5, 11] (11.5, 12.5, 14)cm

7[7½, 7½, 8] (8, 8½, 9)" / 18[19, 19, 20.5] (20.5, 21.5, 23)cm

17¼[19, 21, 22¾] (24½, 26¼, 28¼)" / 44[48.5, 53, 57.5] (62.5, 67, 71.5)cm

14½[15, 15, 15½] (15½, 15½)" / 37[38, 38, 39.5] (39.5, 39.5)cm

21½[22½, 22½, 23½] (23½, 24, 24.5)" / 54.5[57, 57, 59.5] (59.5, 59.5, 61)cm

Stitch Patterns

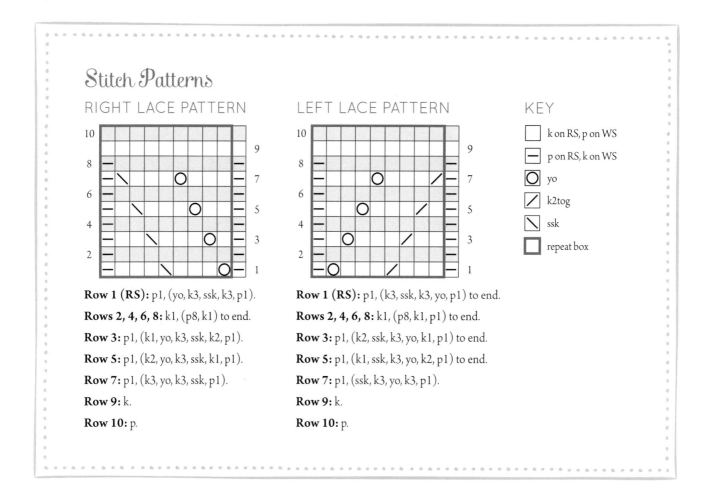

RIGHT LACE PATTERN

Row 1 (RS): p1, (yo, k3, ssk, k3, p1).

Rows 2, 4, 6, 8: k1, (p8, k1) to end.

Row 3: p1, (k1, yo, k3, ssk, k2, p1).

Row 5: p1, (k2, yo, k3, ssk, k1, p1).

Row 7: p1, (k3, yo, k3, ssk, p1).

Row 9: k.

Row 10: p.

LEFT LACE PATTERN

Row 1 (RS): p1, (k3, ssk, k3, yo, p1) to end.

Rows 2, 4, 6, 8: k1, (p8, k1, p1) to end.

Row 3: p1, (k2, ssk, k3, yo, k1, p1) to end.

Row 5: p1, (k1, ssk, k3, yo, k2, p1) to end.

Row 7: p1, (ssk, k3, yo, k3, p1).

Row 9: k.

Row 10: p.

KEY

- ☐ k on RS, p on WS
- ⊟ p on RS, k on WS
- ◯ yo
- ⟋ k2tog
- ⟍ ssk
- ☐ repeat box

Directions

BODY — BACK AND FRONTS
worked flat

With larger needles, CO 197[217, 237, 257] (277, 297, 317) sts.

Set-up row (WS): p3, k1, p2, pm, k1, (p8, k1) 3 times, pm, p129[149, 169, 189] (209, 229, 249) sts, pm, (k1, p8) 3 times, k1, pm, p2, k1, p3.

Row 1 (RS): k3, p1, k2, slm, work from right lace pattern to m, slm, k to marker, slm, work from left lace pattern to m, slm, k2, p1, k3.

Row 2 (WS): p3, k1, p2, slm, work from left lace pattern to m, slm, p to marker, slm, work from right lace pattern to m, slm, p2, k1, p3.

Rep rows 1–2 43[43, 43, 48] (48, 48, 48) more times, ending with row 8 of the 9[9, 9, 10] (10, 10, 10)th repeat of the lace patterns.

Lace shaping section

*Next row (RS): k3, p1, k2, slm, work from right lace pattern to 9 sts before m, pm, k to 3 sts before m, k2tog, p1, slm, m1R, k to m, m1L, slm, p1, ssk, k6, pm, work from left lace pattern to m, slm, k2, p1, k3.

Next row: p3, k1, p2, slm, work from left lace pattern to m, slm, p to 3 sts before m, p2togtbl, k1, slm, m1P, p to m, m1P, slm, k1, p2tog, p to m, slm, work from right lace pattern to m, slm, p2, k1, p3.

Next row: k3, p1, k2, slm, work from right lace pattern to m, slm, k to 3 sts before m, k2tog, p1, slm, m1R, k to m, m1L, slm, p1, ssk, k to m, slm, work from left lace pattern to m, slm, k2, p1, k3.

Rep last 2 rows twice more.

Next row (WS): p3, k1, p2, slm, work from left lace pattern to m, slm, p2togtbl, remove m, m1P, p to m, m1P, remove m, p2tog, slm, work from right lace pattern to m, slm, p2, k1, p3.

Next row: k3, p1, k2, slm, work from *right lace pattern* to m, slm, k to m, slm, work from *left lace pattern* to m, slm, k2, p1, k3.

Next row: p3, k1, p2, slm, work from *left lace pattern* to m, slm, p to marker, slm, work from *right lace pattern* to m, slm, p2, k1, p3.*

Rep last 2 rows 35 more times, ending with row 8 of the 16[16, 16, 17](17, 17, 17)th repeat of the lace patterns from the cast on.

Repeat the lace shaping section from * to * once more.

Continue in patt as established, working a single repeat of the lace patterns between markers and maintaining edging rib, until body measures 14½[15, 15, 15½] (15½, 15½)" / 37[38, 38, 39.5] (39.5, 39.5)cm from CO edge, ending with a WS row.

DIVIDE FRONTS AND BACK AND SHAPE ARMHOLES

Continue working the lace patterns and edging as established while shaping armholes. Do not remove markers.

Next row (RS): work 45[50, 54, 58] (63, 67, 72) sts in patt, slip all sts just worked onto holder or scrap yarn making note of last pattern row worked, BO 12[12, 14, 16] (16, 18, 18) sts, k83[93, 101, 109] (119, 127, 137), slip all stitches just worked onto a separate piece of scrap yarn or spare needle, BO 12[12, 14, 16] (16, 18, 18) sts, work in patt to end. 173[193, 209, 225] (245, 261, 281) sts.

LEFT FRONT

Work left front on 45[50, 54, 58] (63, 67, 72) sts that remain on needles.

Next row (WS): work in patt.

Next row, armhole dec row (RS): k1, ssk, work in patt to end.

Rep last 2 rows 5[6, 7, 8] (10, 11, 12) more times. 39[43, 46, 49] (52, 55, 59) sts rem on left front.

Next row (WS): work in patt.

*Next row, neck dec row (RS):** k to 3 sts before m, k2tog, k1, slm, work in patt to end.

Work in patt for 7[7, 7, 5] (3, 3, 3) rows.

Rep from * 0[2, 2, 4] (6, 7, 8) more times.

Work neck dec row once more. 37[39, 42, 43] (44, 46, 49) sts.

Work even until armhole depth measures 7[7½, 7½, 8] (8, 8½, 9)" / 18[19, 19, 20.5] (20.5, 21.5, 23)cm, ending with a WS row. Break yarn.

Slip 19 sts closest to neck edge to a holder for neck band, and rem 18[20, 23, 24] (25, 27, 30) to a separate holder for shoulder.

RIGHT FRONT

Return sts for right front to needles and, with WS facing, attach yarn to armhole edge of right front piece.

Next row (WS): work in patt.

Next row, armhole dec row (RS): work in patt to 3 sts from end, k2tog, k1.

Rep last 2 rows 5[6, 7, 8] (10, 11, 12) more times. 39[43, 46, 49] (52, 55, 59) sts on right front.

Next row (WS): work in patt.

Next row, neck dec row (RS): work in patt to m, slm, k1, ssk, k to end.

Work in patt for 7[7, 7, 5] (3, 3, 3) rows.

Rep from * 0[2, 2, 4] (6, 7, 8) more times.

Work neck dec row once more. 37[39, 42, 43] (44, 46, 49) sts.

Work even until armhole depth measures 7[7½, 7½, 8] (8, 8½, 9)" / 18[19, 19, 20.5] (20.5, 21.5, 23)cm, ending with WS row. Break yarn.

Slip 19 sts closest to neck edge to a holder for neck band, and rem 18[20, 23, 24] (25, 27, 30) to a separate holder for shoulder.

BACK

Return sts for back to needles and, with WS facing, attach yarn.

Next row (WS): p.

Next row, armhole dec row (RS): k1, ssk, k to last 3 sts, k2tog, k1.

Rep last 2 rows 5[6, 7, 8] (10, 11, 12) more times. 71[79, 85, 91] (97, 103, 111) sts.

Work even until armhole depth measures 7[7½, 7½, 8] (8, 8½, 9)" / 18[19, 19, 20.5] (20.5, 21.5, 23)cm, ending with a WS row.

Next row (RS): k18[20, 23, 24] (25, 27, 30), slip all sts just worked onto scrap yarn, BO centre 35[39, 39, 43] (47, 49, 51) sts, k18[20, 23, 24] (25, 27, 30).

JOIN SHOULDERS

Return 18[20, 23, 24] (25, 27, 30) sts held for left front shoulder to needle, and, with RS held together and WS facing, use a spare needle and the three-needle bind-off to join these with the left back shoulder sts. Return held sts for front and back right shoulder to needles and join in the same way.

NECKBAND

Right band: place 19 right front band sts on smaller needle and, with RS facing, attach yarn. Work in patt as established until the band, when slightly stretched, reaches the middle of the back neck, ending with a WS row. Place sts on hold.

Left band: place 19 left front band sts on smaller needle and, with RS facing, attach yarn. Work in patt as established until the band, when slightly stretched, reaches the middle of the back neck, ending with a WS row.

FINISHING

Join sts for left and right bands with Kitchener stitch. Sew the band to the back neck edge. Weave in loose ends. Block to measurements.

· · · · · · ● · · · · · ·

YARN

A smooth worsted weight yarn with good elasticity and crisp stitch definition. Fiber Optic Yarns Superwash Merino Worsted (100% Superwash Merino wool, 205yds / 180m, 4oz / 114g), shown in Chocolate Kisses.

875[1000, 1100, 1200, 1300] (1400, 1550, 1700, 1850, 2000)yds / 810[900, 975, 1100, 1200] (1300, 1450, 1550, 1700, 1850)m.

NEEDLES AND NOTIONS

US 6 / 4 mm straight or circular needles

Stitch markers

Scrap yarn

Two ½" / 12mm buttons; shown with Shipyard Point Glassworks buttons

GAUGE

20 sts and 28 rows = 4" / 10cm in st st and Dot Stitch.

SIZES

Finished chest circumference: 30½[33½, 35¼, 38½, 41½] (44¾, 48, 51¼, 54½, 57½)" / 77[85.5, 89.5, 97.5, 105.5] (114, 122, 130, 138, 146.5)cm.

Shown in size 38½" with zero ease in the high bust.

Maple Cotton Candy

by Amy Herzog

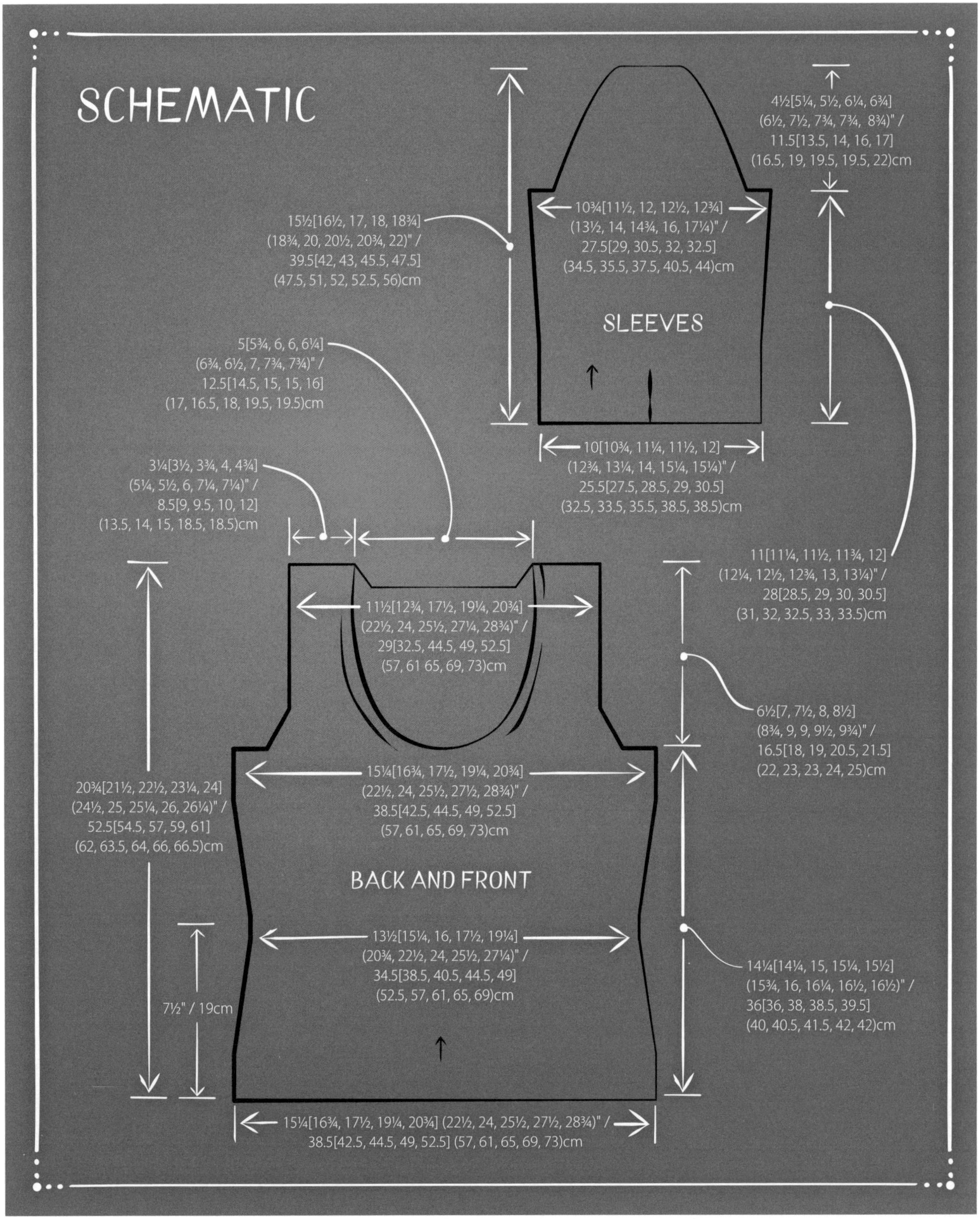
SCHEMATIC
SLEEVES
15½[16½, 17, 18, 18¾] (18¾, 20, 20½, 20¾, 22)" / 39.5[42, 43, 45.5, 47.5] (47.5, 51, 52, 52.5, 56)cm
10¾[11½, 12, 12½, 12¾] (13½, 14, 14¾, 16, 17¼)" / 27.5[29, 30.5, 32, 32.5] (34.5, 35.5, 37.5, 40.5, 44)cm
4½[5¼, 5½, 6¼, 6¾] (6½, 7½, 7¾, 7¾, 8¾)" / 11.5[13.5, 14, 16, 17] (16.5, 19, 19.5, 19.5, 22)cm
10[10¾, 11¼, 11½, 12] (12¾, 13¼, 14, 15¼, 15¼)" / 25.5[27.5, 28.5, 29, 30.5] (32.5, 33.5, 35.5, 38.5, 38.5)cm
11[11¼, 11½, 11¾, 12] (12¼, 12½, 12¾, 13, 13¼)" / 28[28.5, 29, 30, 30.5] (31, 32, 32.5, 33, 33.5)cm
5[5¾, 6, 6, 6¼] (6¾, 6½, 7, 7¾, 7¾)" / 12.5[14.5, 15, 15, 16] (17, 16.5, 18, 19.5, 19.5)cm
3¼[3½, 3¾, 4, 4¾] (5¼, 5½, 6, 7¼, 7¼)" / 8.5[9, 9.5, 10, 12] (13.5, 14, 15, 18.5, 18.5)cm
BACK AND FRONT
11½[12¾, 17½, 19¼, 20¾] (22½, 24, 25½, 27¼, 28¾)" / 29[32.5, 44.5, 49, 52.5] (57, 61 65, 69, 73)cm
6½[7, 7½, 8, 8½] (8¾, 9, 9, 9½, 9¾)" / 16.5[18, 19, 20.5, 21.5] (22, 23, 23, 24, 25)cm
15¼[16¾, 17½, 19¼, 20¾] (22½, 24, 25½, 27½, 28¾)" / 38.5[42.5, 44.5, 49, 52.5] (57, 61, 65, 69, 73)cm
20¾[21½, 22½, 23¼, 24] (24½, 25, 25¼, 26, 26¼)" / 52.5[54.5, 57, 59, 61] (62, 63.5, 64, 66, 66.5)cm
13½[15¼, 16, 17½, 19¼] (20¾, 22½, 24, 25½, 27¼)" / 34.5[38.5, 40.5, 44.5, 49] (52.5, 57, 61, 65, 69)cm
14¼[14¼, 15, 15¼, 15½] (15¾, 16, 16¼, 16½, 16½)" / 36[36, 38, 38.5, 39.5] (40, 40.5, 41.5, 42, 42)cm
7½" / 19cm
15¼[16¾, 17½, 19¼, 20¾] (22½, 24, 25½, 27½, 28¾)" / 38.5[42.5, 44.5, 49, 52.5] (57, 61, 65, 69, 73)cm

Stitch Patterns

Note – stitch counts vary and complete repeats will not always be possible. Knit or purl additional stitches to maintain established pattern.

SEED STITCH
even no. of sts

Row 1 (RS): (k1, p1) to end.

Row 2 (WS): (k1, p1) to end.

DOT STITCH
multiple of 4 sts

Row 1 (RS): (k1, p1, k2) to end.

Row 2: purl.

Row 3 (RS): (k3, p1) to end.

Row 4: purl.

Directions

BACK

CO 76[84, 88, 96, 104] (112, 120, 128, 136, 144) sts. Work even in seed stitch until piece measures 1¼" / 3 cm from CO edge, ending with a WS row.

Next row (RS): work in seed stitch for 8 sts, pm, work in dot stitch to last 8 sts, pm, work in seed stitch to end.

Work in patt until piece measures 2" / 5cm from CO edge, ending with a RS row.

Waist decreases

Note: You will work waist shaping and eliminate the seed stitch panels at the same time. When piece measures 5" / 13cm, remove markers for seed stitch and work all stitches in dot stitch. When shaping the waist, keep the patterned sections aligned as set on either side of the markers.

Next row — place shaping markers (WS): work in patt to m, slm, work 17[20, 21, 24, 27] (29, 32, 35, 37, 40) sts in patt, pm, work 26[28, 30, 32, 34] (38, 40, 42, 46, 48) sts in patt, pm, 17[20, 21, 24, 27] (29, 32, 35, 37, 40) sts in patt, slm, work in patt to end.

Next row (RS): work in patt to 2 sts before first shaping m, ssk, slm, work in patt to second shaping m, slm, k2tog, work in patt to end.

Work 7 rows in patt.

Rep last 8 rows 3 more times. 68[76, 80, 88, 96] (104, 112, 120, 128, 136) sts.

Work even in patt until piece measures 8" / 20.5cm from CO edge, ending with a WS row.

Waist increases

Next row (RS): work in patt to m, m1R, slm, work in patt to m, slm, m1L, work in patt to end.

Work 9 rows even in patt.

Rep last 10 rows 3 more times. 76[84, 88, 96, 104] (112, 120, 128, 136, 144) sts.

Remove markers and work even in patt until piece measures 14¼[14½, 15, 15¼, 15½] (15¾, 16, 16¼, 16½, 16½)" / 36[37, 38, 38.5, 39.5] (40, 40.5, 41.5, 42, 42)cm from CO edge, ending with a WS row.

Shape armholes

Next 2 rows: BO 5[6, 6, 6, 6] (8, 10, 10, 12, 14) sts, work in patt to end.

Next 2 rows: BO 2[2, 2, 2, 4] (4, 6, 8, 8, 10) sts, work in patt to end.

Next row (RS): k1, ssk, work in patt to 3 sts from end, k2tog, k1. Work 1 row in patt.

Rep last 2 rows 1[1, 1, 4, 4] (5, 4, 5, 4, 4) more times: 58[64, 68, 70, 74] (76, 78, 80, 86, 86) sts rem.

Work even until armhole measures 5½[6, 6½, 7, 7½] (7¾, 8, 8, 8½, 8¾)" / 14[15, 16.5, 18, 19] (19.5, 20.5, 20.5, 21.5, 22)cm and piece measures 19¾[20½, 21½, 22¼, 23] (23½, 24, 24¼, 25, 25¼)" / 50[52, 54.5, 56.5, 58.5, 59.5, 61, 61.5, 63.5, 64)cm, ending with a WS row.

Next row (RS): work 18[20, 21, 22, 23] (23, 24, 24, 26, 26) sts in patt, BO centre 22[24, 26, 26, 28] (30, 30, 32, 34, 34) sts, work in patt to end.

You will now work the left shoulder only; place the sts for the right shoulder on scrap yarn if desired.

Left shoulder

Next row (WS): purl.

Next row (RS): k1, ssk, work in patt to end.

Rep last 2 rows once more. 16[18, 19, 20, 21] (21, 22, 22, 24, 24) sts.

Work 2 rows in pattern.

Next row (WS): BO 8[9, 10, 10, 11] (11, 11, 11, 12, 12) sts, work in patt to end.

Work 1 row in patt.

BO rem 8[9, 9, 10, 10] (10, 11, 11, 12, 12) sts.

Right shoulder

With WS facing reattach yarn to held sts.

Next row (WS): purl.

Next row (RS): work in patt to 3 sts from end, k2tog, k1.

Rep last 2 rows once more. 16[18, 19, 20, 21] (21, 22, 22, 24, 24) sts.

Purl 1 row.

Next row (RS): BO 8[9, 10, 10, 11] (11, 11, 11, 12, 12) sts, work in patt to end.

P 1 row.

BO rem 8[9, 9, 10, 10] (10, 11, 11, 12, 12) sts.

FRONT

CO 76[84, 88, 96, 104] (112, 120, 128, 136, 144) sts.

Work as for back, but work shaping marker placement row as follows:
Work in patt to m, slm, work 11[13, 14, 16, 18] (20, 22, 24, 26, 28) sts in patt, pm, work 38[42, 44, 48, 52] (56, 60, 64, 68, 72) sts in patt, pm, work 11[13, 14, 16, 18] (20, 22, 24, 26, 28) sts in patt, slm, work in patt to end.

Continue as for back until piece measures 14¼[14½, 15, 15¼, 15½] (15¾, 16, 16¼, 16½, 16½)" / 36[37, 38, 38.5, 39.5] (40, 40.5, 41.5, 42, 42)cm from CO edge, ending with a RS row.

Next row (WS): p38[42, 44, 48, 52] (56, 60, 64, 68, 72), pm, p to end.

Shape armholes and neck

Next row (RS): BO 5[6, 6, 6, 6] (8, 10, 10, 12, 14) sts, work in patt to 5[6, 6, 6, 6] (7, 7, 7, 8, 8) sts from m, BO centre 10[12, 12, 12, 12] (16, 16, 16, 16, 16) sts removing m, work in patt to end. Place sts for Left Shoulder on scrap yarn if desired; you will now work on Right Shoulder stitches.

Right shoulder

Next row (WS): BO 5[6, 6, 6, 6] (8, 10, 10, 12, 14) sts, work in patt to 3 sts from neck edge, p2tog tbl, p1. 27[29, 31, 35, 39] (39, 41, 45, 47, 49) sts.

Next row (RS): work in patt.

Next row: BO 2[2, 2, 2, 4] (4, 6, 8, 8, 10) sts, p to last 3 sts, p2tog tbl, p1. 24[26, 28, 32, 34] (34, 34, 36, 38, 38) sts.

Note: You will work armhole and neckline decreases at the same time, read through this whole section before continuing.

Use the following decreases to shape the armhole and neck:

On RS rows: decrease at neck edge by beginning the row with k1, ssk; decrease at armhole edge by working to last 3 sts and end k2tog, k1.

On WS rows: decrease at neck edge by working to last 3 sts and end p2tog tbl, p1.

Dec 1 st at armhole edge every RS row 2[2, 2, 5, 5] (6, 5, 6, 5, 5) times and, at the same time:

dec 1 st at neck edge every row 1[1, 1, 1, 2] (1, 1, 1, 2, 2) more times;

then every RS row 2[2, 3, 3, 3] (3, 3, 3, 3, 3) times;

then every other RS row 3[3, 3, 3, 3] (3, 3, 4, 4, 4) times.

16[18, 19, 20, 21] (21, 22, 22, 24, 24) sts remain for shoulder.

Continue even in patt until front measures same as back to beginning of shoulder shaping, ending with a RS row.

Next row (WS): BO 8[9, 10, 10, 11] (11, 11, 11, 12, 12) stitches, work to end.

Work 1 RS row in patt.

BO rem sts.

Left shoulder

With WS facing reattach yarn to 28[30, 32, 36, 40] (40, 42, 46, 48, 50) held sts.

Next row (WS): p1, p2tog, p to end.

Next row (RS): BO 2[2, 2, 2, 4] (4, 6, 8, 8, 10) sts, work in patt to end.

Next row: p1, p2tog, p to end. 24[26, 28, 32, 34] (34, 34, 36, 38, 38) sts.

Use the following decreases to shape the armhole and neck:

On RS rows: decrease at armhole edge by beginning the row with k1, ssk; decrease at neck edge by working to last 3 sts and ending k2tog, k1.

On WS rows: decrease at neck edge by beginning the row with p2tog, p1.

Dec 1 st at armhole edge every RS row 2[2, 2, 5, 5] (6, 5, 6, 5, 5) times, and at the same time:

dec 1 st at neck edge every row 1[1, 1, 1, 2] (1, 1, 1, 2, 2) more times;

then every RS row 2[2, 3, 3, 3] (3, 3, 3, 3, 3) times;

then every other RS row 3[3, 3, 3, 3] (3, 3, 4, 4, 4) times.

16[18, 19, 20, 21] (21, 22, 22, 24, 24) sts remain for shoulder.

Continue even in patt until front measures same as back to beginning of shoulder shaping, ending with a RS row.

Next row (RS): BO 8[9, 10, 10, 11] (11, 11, 11, 12, 12) sts, work in patt to end.

P 1 row.

BO rem sts.

SLEEVES — MAKE TWO

You will start each sleeve with two cuff pieces that will be joined before you start the main part of the sleeve.

CO 26[28, 28, 30, 30] (32, 34, 36, 38, 40) sts. Work in seed stitch for ½" / 1.5cm, ending with a WS row.

Next row (RS): work in seed stitch for 4 sts, work in dot stitch to end. Continue as established until piece measures 3" / 7.5cm from CO edge, ending with a WS row and making note of last row worked. Break yarn, leave cuff sts on needle or put on hold.

CO 26[28, 28, 30, 30] (32, 34, 36, 38, 40) sts.

Work in seed stitch for ½" / 1.5cm, ending with a WS row.

Next row (RS): beg with row 3[1, 1, 3, 3](1, 3, 1, 3, 1) work in dot stitch to last 4 sts, work in seed stitch to end. Continue as established until piece measures same as first cuff piece, being sure to end with a WS row.

Join pieces

Next row (RS): work in patt to end of cuff piece, then join first cuff piece with RS facing and work to end in patt. 52[56, 56, 60, 60] (64, 68, 72, 76, 80) sts rem, with centre 8 in seed stitch. Work even in patt for 1" / 2.5cm. Cuff measures 4" / 10cm from CO edges.

Change to dot stitch and work 4 rows even in patt.

**Next row (RS): k1, m1L, work to last st in patt, m1R, k1.

Work 0[0, 21, 0, 21] (21, 0, 0, 21, 13) rows even in patt.

Rep from ** 0[0, 1, 0, 1] (1, 0, 0, 1, 2) more time(s). 54[58, 60, 62, 64] (68, 70, 74, 80, 86) sts.

Work even in patt until piece measures 11[11¼, 11½, 11¾, 12] (12¼, 12½, 12¾, 13, 13¼)" / 28[28.5, 29, 30, 30.5] (31, 32, 32.5, 33, 33.5) cm from CO edge, ending with a WS row.

Shape sleeve cap

Next 2 rows: BO 5[6, 6, 6, 6] (8, 10, 10, 12, 14) sts, work in patt to end.

Next 2 rows: BO 2[2, 2, 2, 4] (4, 6, 8, 8, 10) sts, work in patt to end.

Work 5 rows even.

Next row — dec row (RS): k1, ssk, work in patt to 3 sts from end, k2tog, k1.

Rep last 6 rows 0[1, 1, 2, 3] (5, 6, 6, 6, 5) more times;

then rep dec row every 4th row 0[0, 0, 0, 1] (0, 0, 0, 1, 3) times;

then every RS row 8[8, 9, 9, 6] (1, 1, 2, 0, 0) times.

BO 2[2, 2, 2, 2] (3, 3, 3, 3, 3) sts at the beginning of the next 4 rows.

BO rem 14[14, 14, 14, 14] (18, 18, 18, 18, 24) sts.

FINISHING

Wet block all sweater pieces to match measurements as shown. Join shoulder seams using mattress stitch.

Set in sleeves and sew using mattress stitch. Sew side and underarm seams using mattress stitch, leaving the bottom 5" / 13cm of sides open for vents.

Neckline

CO 8 sts to working needles.

With CO sts on right-hand needle, begin approximately 2" / 5cm above the bound-off sts of the left front neck, and pick up and knit 1 st for every st and approximately 2 sts for every 3 rows around neckline, being sure to have an even number.

Work even in seed stitch until neck trim measures 1" / 2.5cm. BO all sts.

Overlap neckline "tab" and final 2" of neckline sts as shown, and sew buttons in place. Weave in ends.

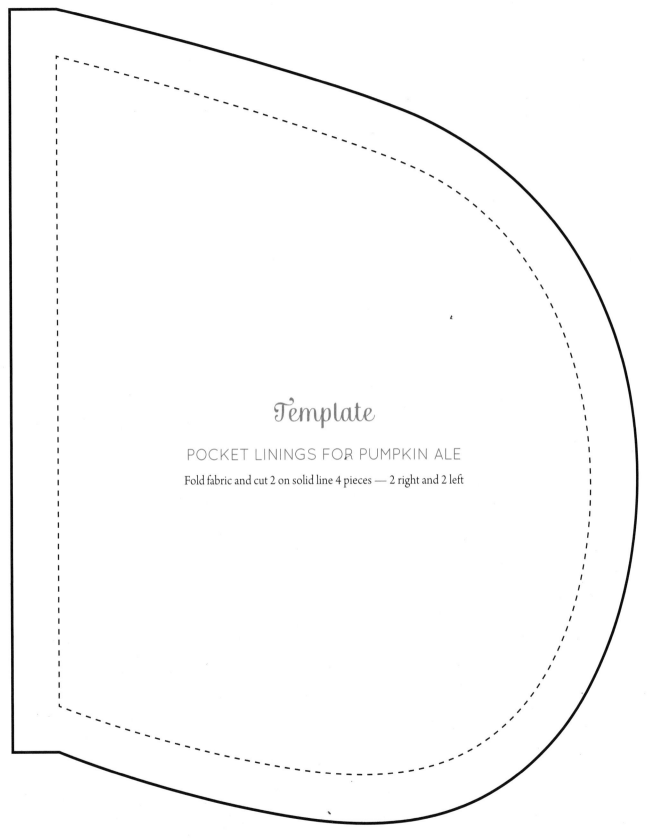

Template

POCKET LININGS FOR PUMPKIN ALE

Fold fabric and cut 2 on solid line 4 pieces — 2 right and 2 left

Sources

YARNS

Jenny at the Fair
Starcroft Fiber Mill
www.starcroftfiber.com

Dutchess
Shelridge Farm
www.shelridge.com

Sugarleaf and Pippin
Green Mountain Spinnery
www.spinnery.com

Beekman Tavern
Foxhill Farm
Rhinebeck and other festivals

Pumpkin Ale
Miss Babs
www.missbabs.com

Aunt Fred
Briar Rose Fibers
www.briarrosefibers.net

Apple Cider Donut
Bartlettyarns
www.bartlettyarns.com

Mulberry Street
The Verdant Gryphon
www.verdantgryphon.com

Artichoke French
Jill Draper Makes Stuff
www.etsy.com/shop/jilldrapermakesstuff

Spring Brook
Bijou Basin Ranch
www.bijoubasinranch.com

Maple Cotton Candy
Fiber Optic Yarns
www.kimberbaldwindesigns.com

NOTIONS

Sugarleaf
Toggle buttons
Melissa Jean Designs
www.melissajean.net

Maple Cotton Candy
Buttons
Shipyard Point Glassworks
www.spglassworks.com

ABOUT THE AUTHOR

Ysolda Teague is a Scottish designer who has published popular knitting patterns in Twist Collective and Knitty, as well as three books in her Whimsical Little Knits series, a pattern collection and resource book Little Red in the City and an accessory collection in collaboration with Fyberspates, Saturday Treat. Her many other patterns are available on her website, www.ysolda.com, and in yarn stores. She lives and works in Edinburgh but loves to travel, especially when it means meeting the people who make her patterns.

ACKNOWLEDGEMENTS

This book wouldn't have been possible without everyone featured in it; designers and yarn companies alike committed their time, passion, and brilliant smiles to bring it to life. My heartfelt thanks to all of them. There are also a few people not featured on these pages whose work behind the scenes to make them as beautiful as they are deserves recognition.

Kristi Porter took a dozen patterns in different voices and made them fit smoothly together, wrangling unruly numbers and out of control charts. When, right at the end, I was overwhelmed by writing the blurb, you made it seem simple. Jo Kelly showed up at the studio with coffee in hand, enthusiastically discussed split infinitives, American versus British spelling and tamed my eccentric punctuation. Mary-Heather Cogar's valuable advice helped to shape much of the writing and her initial enthusiasm had a great deal to do with the fact that the book happened at all.

Visiting mills and the island shearing were some of the best things that happened because of this book, and I'm so grateful to Mary Jane, Gudrun, Gale and Ellen for making those visits possible — one of these days I'll learn to drive myself but I'll miss your company on road trips. Thank you to everyone at Green Mountain Spinnery and Bartlettyarns for letting me poke around, interrupt your work, and for answering my endless questions cheerfully. Thank you to Jani and the Wakemans for welcoming a stranger with open arms, appreciating my clumsy help with the sheep and barely even noticing my lens.

Most of all, thank you to my assistants Bex and Saz. Thank you Bex for making sure the photoshoot went smoothly, the patterns were accurate, for working horrific hours at evenings and weekends, and for always doing the dishes so that the studio isn't a pigsty. Thank you Sarah for keeping all of the tedious parts of the business running so well that I rarely have to think of them, and for your extremely motivating desire to knit all of the patterns. Thank you, too, to Erin, my occasional stateside assistant: your help lugging everything around, tracking down designers and holding reflectors at the photoshoot was invaluable, and your test-knitting turned good patterns into great.